YOU KNOW ... AY

A Memoir Presaging ...

Elizabeth Miles Graham

NEW YORK, NY

You Know What They Say
By Elizabeth Miles Graham

ISBN: 978-1-7360288-0-3

Edited by Susan Toth
Cover Art by HJC
Interior Design by Marty Marsh

Manufactured in the United States of America

Elizabeth Miles Graham
New York, NY

Dedication

For my daughter... my love and my light.

Disclaimer

This memoir is based in part on actual events of sexual abuse, discrimination, and retaliation by male co-workers that occurred in the life of the author. Some names, places, dates, events, and dialogue have been changed to preserve the privacy of the people involved. The author's purpose of this memoir is to promote the awareness and prevention of sexual abuse, discrimination, and retaliation against women in the workplace.

Introduction

It is the attack of the cliché. You cannot avoid it. "Well, you know what they say..." Who the hell are "they"? And why should we be listening to "them" anyway? These sayings pop up everywhere throughout life. It seems like when you are going through a particularly difficult time, you can be overwhelmed by them. You know what they say, "If life hands you lemons, make lemonade," or "What goes around comes around," or "Everything happens for a reason." Oh, here's a good one, "Blow it out your..." Never mind.

You hear it from close friends, relatives, acquaintances, and on the rare dreaded occasion, you even hear it from strangers. Yes, people who know absolutely nothing about you, your life, or what you are going through at the time, feel the need to respond to a brow crinkle or a somber sigh. Now you have to admit that sometimes it is your fault that people feel obliged to comment since you advertise your misery with these random physical or vocal indicators. And oftentimes, people mean well. However, when you do feel this way, the last thing you want to hear from anyone, no less a random passerby, is some cheesy little saying that actually makes you want to gag. I mean seriously, what is preventing you from gripping the base of that intrusive person's neck and squeezing it so tightly that you expect to have to duck for fear of getting hit by flying eyeballs?

I can recall a specific incident like this. It was an errand day and my last stop was the dry cleaners. It was about a hundred degrees outside, which means two hundred degrees in the teeny little shoebox of a place. I have a very low tolerance for heat as it

7

is, and it didn't help that there were about twenty-seven other people, with either their filthy stinky clothes in tow or their little pink tickets that doubled as fans, who decided to make their errand day the same day as mine. Fanning themselves with the dry-cleaning receipts; I mean, really, they would be more success-ful if they just wiped the greasy sweat from their faces with the darn things. Ugh. It's like there should be a city-wide bulletin board with a huge errand schedule on it. Everyone, divided up by neighborhood, is assigned a color. There are a total of seven col-ors and one day for each color. You and your color can run your errands only on those days. Anyway, I must not have appeared too thrilled to be there. When I was finished and tried to squeeze my way through the crowd and back outside to the relief of the hundred-degree heat to get a nice deep breath of comparatively fresh crisp air, this woman looks over at me and says, "Well, you know what they say, tomorrow's another day, right?"

Where do I even begin? Are you kidding me? Why, by any stretch of her imagination, would she think that it would be a good idea to say something like that to me at that time? I know it sounds terribly rude of me. I should be thrilled that there is actually one friendly person left in New York. The truth is that I was not always this crabby. I used to love people. In my eyes, human beings in general were good. Friendly ones even moved up in status to "better than just plain old good." I always gave peo-ple the benefit of the doubt, unless they proved me wrong.

A few people did prove me wrong. I hate to admit it, but I was quite gullible. With this incredible sense of goodness towards mankind came a certain naiveté. I reeked of it. That is when things went downhill for me. My life changed dramatically. And through this life change, I learned that the annoying little saying, a.k.a. the "cliché," actually was my ally.

8

Part One

Every Cloud Has A Silver Lining

Chapter 1

It was the early 2000s, back when I was an eager beaver of a thing in my twenties. I thought I had it all. A business degree from a terrific college, an incredibly prestigious job, a great family, awesome friends, and an apartment in the city with my very best friend of twenty plus years.

Living with Jill was like having a little piece of home with me in this new, big, scary, strange place. She and I grew up in the same neighborhood in an upper middle-class suburb of northern New Jersey. It was a great place to live. Our block alone had seven families on it all with kids ranging in age over a twelve-year span. We grew up together in a time and a place where moms were homemakers and we could play outside unsupervised until all hours without any tangible fear of becoming a kidnap statistic. Jill is one year older than I am. She has two younger brothers, Frankie and Sean. I have one older sister, Heather, who was always so mature and beyond her years that she never hung out with us younger ones. She wasn't even really considered one of the "neighborhood kids." She graduated high school and went off to college while I was still in elementary school, eighth grade to be exact. I'll never forget that year because that was the year Jill started high school. I thought my life was over. Heather and Jill both left me at the same time. Jill and I drifted apart over the next couple of years. I started at a private high school that next fall and then we went to our respective colleges. It was my winter break of freshman year, Jill's sophomore year, that we reconnected. Our parents were still very close, and her folks were having a Christmas party that we were all invited to. Jill and I snuck a few wine coolers up to her room and reminisced the night away. We ended up crying and swearing to one another that we would never drift apart again. We certainly kept our promises. The next few years, even though we were at different colleges, consisted of a lot of late night phone calls and inseparable summers.

I guess I knew all along that Jill and I would never really part as friends. I am sure our parents remaining very close influenced our decision to reconnect. In fact, much of our neighborhood was still intact. Six houses on our one block were still occupied by their original owners. The neighborhood was a lot quieter since most of the kids were moved out, but still in many ways, it was the same. I had suspected that within the next few years, the streets would be filled with the neighborhood kids' children visiting their grandparents. Jill's parents, Dr. and Mrs. Coyle, moved in to the brand new development exactly one month after my parents did almost thirty years ago. I recall one time about fifteen years after we moved in, when my father's practice and the economy were booming, my parents tossing around the idea of an "upgrade." For a fleeting moment, they imagined themselves in a neighborhood a little bit newer, trendier, and fancier, but then couldn't imagine themselves without the Coyles, or the rest of the families on our block, for that matter. My folks were extremely modest people, especially my dad. "Upgrades" really weren't their thing. Friendships and memories were more important to them than fancy cars and additional fireplaces. Our house was big and nice enough as it was and they both knew that leaving it would be ridiculous.

Jill was always fun to be around. She was very kooky. She always seemed like she was performing. She was very loud and over-enunciated everything. She spoke like a game show host and was one of those people others referred to as the mayor. She was the mayor of the neighborhood, at school, at her work, and eventually the mayor of our building. She knew everyone and their apartment numbers. I was a very shy girl when I was younger, so she and I were a perfect pair. She would tell jokes and stories and be the center of attention and I would make sure I laughed, listened, or signaled secretly if she had a booger hanging out of her nose or spinach in her teeth while everyone was looking at her.

I didn't have the confidence to be like Jill. I was always one of the smarter kids in school, but I couldn't compete with the absolute best and brightest, nor was I ever the prettiest. As most pre-teens and teens do, I based my self-worth on what I thought was "wrong" with me instead of acknowledging what I was capable of and being proud of myself for that. Eventually, though, some self-esteem developed as I got older. That might have been because just before high school, I got contact lenses so the coke bottle glasses I wore were gone, completed my four years of retainers, head gears, and braces, and got an early teen nose job. Yes, if I recall correctly, as I washed away all of my nerdiness, some of my insecure feelings went with it. Because my appearance changed in a way that society considered "for the better," people responded to me in a more positive way. Thus, I became more confident. It was a very good thing that I developed this shred of self-esteem, albeit based on superficial things, because without it, I don't think I would have made it through the most difficult time of my life. In some ways, though, I wish I always had it more ingrained in me. Then I probably could have avoided some if not all of the most difficult time of my life.

I was very blessed in the friend department. Jill was my oldest friend. But she was not my only close friend. I had managed to stay in touch with a group of nearest and dearest from high school. The girls were Marissa and me and the guys were Steve, Jim, and Brian. Brian's younger sister, Kristin, was good friends with us, too, even though she didn't graduate with us. We were initially part of a larger crowd back in the day, but the ones who off and married immediately after their respective college graduations sort of drifted. They weren't at the same stage in life that the rest of us were. We were still going out every weekend, partying, and spending money. We were living it up as swinging singles. We didn't have any major responsibilities, financial or otherwise. Don't get me wrong, we didn't snub the marrieds. We'd hang out with them from time to time; just not as often as with each other. The group of single friends was able to tighten that bond all over again when we each returned to the New York City metropolitan area after our four years apart.

We all went away to school, except Marissa. She went to a community college that had a great nursing program. She was really smart but very much a klutz and very easy to make fun of. Trust me, the guys took full advantage. She had this intensely high-pitched voice that sometimes made the hair on the back of your neck stand at attention. It was as annoying as nails on a chalkboard but not as screechy. It almost sounded like a character from a children's movie or television show. She spoke very slowly by dragging out every word, so that didn't help either. Anytime she said something stupid, which was pretty often, the guys would go on hour-long rampages imitating her. I had to admit, I felt so bad laughing sometimes, but it was really funny. She was always a good sport and could laugh at herself, though. Besides, I myself was no stranger to being the butt of the guys' jokes either. She and I were the closest of our high school friends. We first met even before school started freshman year at cheerleading tryouts and were really close ever since. I couldn't believe that we were all still so close. It was rare. And not a one of us took our friendships for granted. Random segments of our group would be hanging out at any given time during a weekend. We all communicated through one another. We worked well together. Don't get me wrong, there was a lot of drama at times. But for the most part, the drama was created by the girls so that the guys could have something to make fun of us for. Jill even fit in with my high school friends. Sometimes, since it had been so long that they've known her, they'd forgotten that she didn't go to high school with us.

So, I had my great friends and the great apartment in the city. Okay, okay, so the apartment wasn't that great. It was actually even smaller than that drycleaning place that I told you about before. But it was rat- and cockroach-free, it had solid walls, a full bathroom and well, kind of a kitchen. The whole kitchen part didn't matter to my roommate Jill or me. The place really wasn't meant for two people to live. But it was so expensive to rent a two-bedroom apartment in the city and since we were both just starting out on our own, we decided to pretend that I was renting the alcove studio by myself. Her name wasn't even on the lease. Everybody lies to get an apartment in the city. It was no big deal. That's how the average person can afford to live there. I have a friend who is paying $1200/month (very cheap) in a rent-controlled apartment on the Upper East side but has to have a P.O. Box for his mail because if anyone were to find out that his cousin's friend actually moved out six years earlier, they'd all be in trouble. He even has to mail his cousin's friend some of her mail that still gets delivered there.

Anyway, Jill and I honestly didn't think it would be that bad. What did we know? We didn't care. We were just happy to move out of our homes in the New Jersey suburbs. We didn't mind that the place was so small. All that mattered is that it was ours. At that time, we would've moved into a cardboard box under the George Washington Bridge if someone would have allowed us. As long as we had that city address, we felt like big time. We are both really little anyway. I am 5'2" on a good day and Jill stands a mere inch and a half taller. We don't take up that much space. That was our logic when I agreed to sign a year lease.

The apartment was located in an "up and coming" neighborhood on the West side. "Up and coming" translated into "pretty dangerous and very run down, so it can't get any worse, it can only improve at some point in the distant future." What a joke. Combined, the two of us had enough clothing and shoes to dress a small country. And since closet space is as rare as a parking space in the city, every single piece of furniture turned into a dresser. As if the place wasn't cramped enough, we had to go and throw piles of clothes on top of the couch back, the coffee table and even the TV stand. It was a 500-square-foot place. The living area was long and narrow, shaped like a rectangle with one window and a radiator along the far wall. That radiator must have been there for the "charm" affect because it didn't seem to work, ever. The alcove was off on the far right. We each put a single bed on either side of the alcove against each wall, thus instantly creating the college dorm room effect. There was only enough room left for one nightstand each. We placed our nightstands in between our beds against the back wall. There were no windows in the alcove, which one would normally think is bad thing. Not in this case. The more wall space we had, the better.

Since we could not fit our dressers in the alcove area, we had them back against the foot of our beds, which made them clearly visible no matter where you stood in the entire apartment, including in the bathroom. Oh, the bathroom! The bathroom was insanely small. It didn't even have a door. We hung a shower curtain in the spot that was supposed to be a doorway. Picture the smallest bathroom you've ever seen and reduce its size by about two square feet. Whoever created this pseudo-bathroom should have just dug three holes in the ground; two with faucets and one with a flusher.

Aside from the dressers poking out into the main living area, Jill and I were very creative and maximized the space to make it a great room. Almost directly across from the entrance to the alcove and on an angle, we had one adorable moss green couch that was so soft and fluffy we literally sank into it. We also had an equally adorable coffee table and a smaller version of it as a side table. The matching chair was supposed to come with an ottoman but, of course, there wasn't enough room for it, so we didn't bother getting it. There was a tiny two-person table, basically in the middle of the room, which was handed down to us from Jill's parents. The tabletop folded in half when it wasn't in use to conserve space. The matching chairs were actually too big, so we bought some cheap folding chairs to complete the set.

It was small and bursting at the seams with all of our stuff, but it served its purpose. And once I saw Elizabeth Graham on that mailbox label, I got goose bumps. This was it. I was on my own. I was all grown up. It was exciting but scary at the same time, just as leaving the home I'd been raised in my entire life was bittersweet. I felt bad for a moment because Jill unfortunately couldn't see her name on that mailbox label, since she wasn't on the lease. She claimed that it didn't matter to her. I could tell that I was a bit more excited by that than she was. I was always very easily amused though.

Chapter 2

So there I was, living it up in the Big Apple with my best friend, loving life. We had been living in the apartment about two years or so when I got word that the position I applied and interviewed for at work was all mine. I couldn't believe it. I beat out 13 other candidates. It was a job that I never dreamed I would be able to get but took a shot because I really had nothing to lose. The opportunity was once in a lifetime for me and I jumped at the chance. I was huge. I was on fire. I was working on the trading floor at a major financial institution. It wasn't the trading floor of the Stock Exchange or any of those larger exchange trading floors; it was our company's own version of those types of places. We will call the company Bigg, Swingin, Johnson and Co., or simply, BSJ & Co. I would never have called it this at the time I was hired, of course, but things change.

Anyway, I had been at the company about five years. My latest position had been a Sales Assistant when I was hired to be a Sales Trader. I got my first interview at the firm right out of college through our job search program at school. I had a 3.6 GPA and graduated with honors. I interviewed very well and looked great on paper. I have to say that I really did pay my dues during those three years as a Sales Assistant. I knew the business inside and out and had a complete understanding of how our desk functioned. Everyone who worked with me liked me and knew I had a very strong work ethic. I was tremendously helpful and always took initiative. I asked the right questions at the right time. I took my job very seriously. I was so proud of myself and how far I had come. I thrived on the fact that I shocked the hell out of people who didn't really know me or hadn't seen me in a while when I would tell them what I did for a living. At first glance, well, at second, third, and fourth too, I didn't look much like some financial whiz. As I mentioned earlier, I am very petite. I had a very youthful, attractive face (kudos to my holy trinity of beautification... in the name of the ophthalmologist, the orthodontist, and the plastic surgeon, amen) with brown eyes and long, straight blonde hair. I actually thought of cutting it when I graduated from college because it was supposedly more professional. If I had trouble finding a job, I might have eventually, but I didn't need to. It was always well groomed and shiny or tied back in a ponytail, so it looked impeccably neat. Actually, I looked impeccable from head to toe most work days. I took pride in how I looked. I was a professional. It was exciting to dress grown up.

I remember the Sunday night before I started my new position. I made Jill watch *Working Girl* with me. I loved that movie and it got me all pumped up for my big promotion. There was something about that Carly Simon song that really got me fired up. It worked, really. I couldn't wait to enter into this new phase of my career. I knew the people that I'd be working with and had the utmost respect for the management team. They were a brilliant group. One manager in particular was my mentor. Her name was Roberta and from day one she took me under her wing. She wasn't threatened by me or anything like that, which was rare. I came to learn that most women where I worked were underhanded and often felt threatened by other women. There were so few of us, why couldn't we all have just stuck together and supported one another? But Roberta was different. She took extra time with me and had infinite patience with my many questions. She was very proud of me and told me so on several occasions. Everyone knew that Roberta was a terrific woman to work for and she knew it, too. From what I had heard, it was very rare to find a manger like her. I was very lucky. I barely slept a wink that night before my first day. I was too excited. It was the exact same feeling I would get on Christmas Eve when I was little. Instead of awaiting a Barbie Dream House, I was anticipating my jump in salary and my big fat bonus.

When I arrived at work that first morning, I couldn't believe that I was in the first elevator bank taking it only to the tenth floor. I was getting off on the trading floor where all the big shooters were. I wasn't going up to that teeny cubicle anymore. Even though I had been an assistant to the Sales Trading Desk, we peons didn't get to enjoy the trading floor hullabaloo. We were one flight up and had to do all the running back and forth fifty times a day. It was like a status thing. You were nothing if you didn't own real estate on the tenth floor. Apparently, up until I started at the firm, assistants were seated with the traders. But it was decided that those seats were way too valuable and needed to be occupied by the masters of the universe. Huh, now I was one of them. I had walked onto that floor thousands of times before, but this time it was different. I was there to stay. My heart was pounding so hard I swore it was popping through my chest like you would see in cartoons. It was an amazing feeling. I was overwhelmed with excitement.

The trading floor was like a zoo, literally. Bulls, bears, pigs... oops, sorry, did I say pigs? Anyway, it was extremely loud and if you could watch it from above at a distance it would look a lot like an ant colony. Lots of little people running around in all different directions, each serving a specific purpose. There were dozens of different phones ringing and dozens of different people yelling across the room to one another. It seemed like chaos, but there was actually a method to this madness. Every group was seated together by the product that it traded, with the main walkway straight up the middle of the trading floor. Off to each side were rows of long desks, with each individual desk only about three feet wide. Each trader had two raised computer screens, with a touch screen phone bank underneath. Call volume was extremely high most days, so our desk was assigned about twelve phone lines that we all shared. If someone was calling for me, anyone on our desk could answer it. That's one reason why there was so much shouting, even though they were such tight quarters that people appeared to be sitting on top of one another. The rows were tiered, like in an auditorium. In fact, it was very much like an auditorium because of its high ceiling — the more room for all the hot air that flew around that place, the better. If the raucousness or the thousands of tiny numbers and charts blinking and jumping across the hundreds of computer and phone screens weren't enough to give you a headache, the lighting sure would. Industrial-sized fluorescent lights beamed throughout the room. It probably took more energy to light one of these things than it did to light Memphis, Tennessee. Shockingly, over all of that other noise, you could still hear the buzz of those stinking lights. The room had floor-to-ceiling windows along its perimeter, so the lights seemed even more excessive. But this was the place where I was going to spend my ten-hour days for the next God knows how many years and I wouldn't have wanted it any other way. It was awesome.

The following six months were just as I had expected. They were tremendously challenging but thrilling nonetheless. I had ridiculously long hours but since the day was jam packed and nonstop, time flew by. I hit the ground running and never looked back. I got great feedback on my performance from Roberta and the other managers. I had built up an incredible account book and was trading hundreds of thousands to millions of dollars a day. I had a big bright future ahead of me and I couldn't wait to face every minute of it. I was flying high and enjoying the ride.

The days were often long because I usually arrived early to settle in and read up on the day's events. Several foreign markets were already trading, so I would check on what was happening in those places and read my *Wall Street Journal* cover to cover while drinking my coffee. I wanted to make sure that I was up to speed on everything that was going on so I could anticipate what was ahead for the US markets. At the end of the trading day, I often stayed late to confirm all the trades went through properly. This was mostly the responsibility of the trading assistants, but since I just came from that position, I didn't mind doing some of the work myself. I wanted to be certain that there were never any errors. We had two different computer systems. One was our internal company-wide system, and those trades had to match up to the other system our clients used. I'm sure nowadays the systems are more sophisticated and efficient, but that was how we processed trades and I didn't mind doing it.

Some of the day's work was after hours. It is very common in any field of business to have to entertain clients. I always had a nice time doing so under Roberta and our previous managers. These outings consisted of great drinks, great dinners, and, of course, great company. I was very good at building relationships with my clients. I proved that I knew the business well and took my job very seriously. Out at dinners, these clients saw a side of me that they definitely appreciated. I was easygoing and light-hearted. I added a human element to our relationship that they often admitted they never felt with other traders they worked with. I wasn't trying to act superior towards anyone. I was intelligent without bragging, confident without being arrogant, and assertive without being aggressive. Roberta often complimented me on my people skills and my ability to communicate very well. And with each comment came a little more self confidence that made me progress even more. Roberta always introduced me to our clients and referred to me as her equal. She knew that it would give our clients peace of mind that they were working with someone who was extremely capable. If she trusted me to do a good job, so should they. They did, and I didn't disappoint. I knew I was in good hands with Roberta as my mentor, but I might not have known just how good I had it, and how much that would soon change.

Chapter 3

The reorganization rumors began circulating just before the holidays that year. I had breezed by my ninety-day probationary period and smoothly sailed past the half year mark. At first, I wasn't too worried about these rumors because I didn't think that I would be directly affected. Besides, I had just gotten my performance evaluation and I had far exceeded my objectives, thus awarding me a handsome bonus, even though I had been in my new position a mere nine months.

Well I couldn't have been more wrong. Our new head of the division came on board in January. He had big plans to "trim the fat" and make BSJ & Co. an efficient, fine-tuned machine. He brought in people from his former company and dispersed them throughout. They were his disciples and they were all in charge where it counted. Out of the three managers on our desk, two were sent to Florida and Roberta was shipped off to Chicago. I can't say that I totally understood the logic of this reorganization at the time. We were performing very well, and we had the numbers to back it up. At her farewell dinner, Roberta tried to explain it to me as diplomatically as she could, but I still couldn't really follow her. My naiveté got in the way. Finally, she succumbed to "Que sera sera." That was the first cliché that slapped me upside the head and knocked me on my butt. She was married to a man with a very successful career here in New York and had three kids, two in high school and one in college. It didn't matter to anyone that she had been at the firm twenty-three years and she was expected to take a pay cut at this new position. It took me a while to realize that they were just trying to get her to resign. That is what was meant by "trimming the fat." Attempt to push out the loyal people who made this place what it was and replace them with younger, cheaper employees who didn't understand the values of the firm. Actually, they didn't even need to because that was when the firm lost all of its values.

I cried when I had to say goodbye to Roberta. I knew we'd keep in touch, but I also knew that my job wasn't going to be the same again. I wasn't even too sure if I was going to like it at all anymore. From what I had gathered, things were going to be changing quite a bit. Two other traders on our desk were asked to leave along with the managers but weren't given the choice to uproot their entire lives if they so desired.

When the new managers first met with us before they even started working with us, I could tell immediately that they had that "disciple" mentality. I hadn't quite realized the full-on "fraternity" mentality right away, unfortunately. The three new gentlemen were our manager, Todd Stanley, our director, Richard Miller, and their direct boss, Clark Brewster. They claimed to all be excited to turn our team around and maximize on its potential. They were so full of crap. They were all up each other's butts. It was obvious that they wanted to just make themselves more money. They strutted around talking about how successful THEY all were at their previous company and what THEY accomplished. It seemed as if they wanted to just take over and not incorporate anything about how we did business. They wanted to implement their tactics and have us simply follow suit. Maybe I was so cynical because I was bitter about Roberta and the other managers leaving. Cynicism was new to me at the time, though, and I didn't know how to deal with it. So I followed the rules and played along.

Clark Brewster hadn't been seen since that first meeting. We heard, through Rich and Todd, about his expectations of us. He never met with us directly again. He didn't have the time to deal with anyone not in management. He was always in meetings with the CEO or at huge important conferences. Some of these meetings were totally top secret, too. It was completely ridiculous. I mean really, we were all trained to believe that this guy was the most important person to walk through the doors of this place. I think it was an intimidation tactic. He was like the Wizard of Oz. It was very difficult for anyone in our group to get a meeting with him. Of course, you had to go through his assistant first. Let me tell you, she better have gotten a huge bonus for having to come up with some of the crap excuses for where he was that she did. She was very creative.

When I say that I followed the rules, I meant that I kept my mouth shut and "yessed" Todd and Rich to death. Todd would ask the same few guys to talk during the morning meetings. Two of these guys were from our original group and two came in with Todd and the new team. This was a big deal because Rich didn't sit on the Trading Floor, so he didn't witness anything first hand. He had an office three floors up but came downstairs every day for this morning meeting. This meant that if Todd selected you to speak at the meeting, Rich would see you as an integral part of the group. Todd didn't select these men because they were the best and brightest. He fed them the information to talk about. I honestly didn't think anything of it at first. Sometimes, Rich would come down to Todd's desk and tell Todd to, "Round up the guys" and they would all go to Rich's office for a quick meeting. It was always the same few men. Early on, I didn't know how or why these guys were "selected." They were not stand-out performers. But I could see these same few men becoming Todd's favorites.

Rich and Todd just appeared to be arrogant and overeager. It was obvious that they ate, slept, and breathed this job. They both had wives and families to go home to, but Todd never did. Rich was very stoic and serious. He was all business. Todd had a bit of a likeable personality. He was the approachable one. He used that to his advantage quite often. It was a way for him to get people like me to do things for him that weren't necessarily in our job descriptions. Things like ordering his lunch and booking his travel arrangements became a regular part of my daily responsibilities. He should have had an assistant for things like this but didn't. I guess it was more economical to have someone already on the payroll take on these duties. At least at that point anyway. He mentioned to me that he was awaiting approval from the higher ups to assign him an assistant. But in the meantime, he would smile his cute, crooked smile, and I would give in. I was having a very difficult time trying to juggle my accounts and the random stuff that Todd had me do for him. Actually, after the first couple of months, he had moved my seat so that I was right next to him. He sat in the last row of our group, highest tier all the way on the end. He chose that seat because it overlooked everyone in the group and was right against the windows. Window seats were the most coveted. I then had the second-best seat possible. It was actually pretty neat. I felt really important, even though some of the tasks I was required to perform were rather menial. He really liked me, though, and that was so important to me. I thought that we were forming a great professional relationship. He made it seem like he respected me tremendously and knew how smart I was and how well I did my job. I believed him. I was such a dumb ass.

Todd had this rare charm about him, and I fell for it. He wasn't all that attractive, maybe average, but he had a way of making you feel very smart, accomplished, and special. I came to find out that this was far from what he actually thought of me. He praised me and complimented me. And I thought it was all for real, but it wasn't. He was tall and had a very nice build. I never understood how he could keep that build either. He ate crap and I knew because I was the one ordering and fetching his meals for him. He never worked out nor did he ever have the stamina or desire to. But still, he won me over. And he did a damn good job of it too. I was the moron who let him, but we won't get into that just yet. He would woo me as if he was trying to court me. He'd wink at me and throw me "that" smile when he asked me to do something for him that was just completely beyond even the most menial of chores. I guess that was the only way he knew how to get women to do things for him. This, by the way, was why he thought women were around at all, to do things for him. Women were not corporate climbers and most definitely not traders at major Wall Street firms. He certainly succeeded at putting me in my place. I initially considered us colleagues. Shame on me. It was like the old school mentality of where a woman's place should be except it was the twenty first century. I never could understand, though, how he got his male followers on board. Did he wink and smile at them too? Were they all closeted gay men? Actually, now that I think about it, that is a very good possibility.

I was first taken aback when I noticed that Todd would ask me to get something done for him immediately and in return he would field my calls, pretending that he was doing me a favor. A few times I would hear him on the phone with my accounts telling them that he was my manager and that they could deal with him also. Seemed harmless, right? Wrong. After a while, these accounts just started calling him directly, completely bypassing me. He was literally stealing my accounts from right under my nose and I let him. I was in an awkward position because I felt like I couldn't say anything to him. He once said to me that he was still giving me credit for every trade that he did under accounts that were initially mine. I believed him. He said that the group couldn't run smoothly if I wasn't doing the important things I was doing. Personally, I didn't see how finding a spectacular country club for us to have our golf outing was more important than making money for the firm, but what did I know? I wasn't management. Nor was I in any position to object to what management was doing. Eventually, Rich, too, had me doing similar tasks for him. And why shouldn't he? I had gotten to know the people in our corporate travel department so well. I knew the ins and outs of booking a car service and making reservations for client dinners. Oddly enough at first, I felt so important doing these things for them. They both had such a way of making this work I did seem like the most important thing. They praised me, which was actually extraordinarily patronizing, but I was completely responsive to their praise. I didn't see it. I could kick myself now, of course, but at the time, I could never have imagined that these intelligent grown men were screwing me over.

Forget the idea of grown men. The atmosphere of our group was like a John Hughes movie. Total high school complete with cliques of the popular and the geeks. Todd was like the captain of the football team and a small group of his disciples was forming. It was so ridiculous. Where you came from, what kind of car you drove, and what your father did for a living all mattered. Obviously, the ones whose dads were CEOs of various companies or held seats on the NY Stock Exchange or were big government power players were among the popular crowd. These folks were like the ones in high school who ran the place. They were the heads of every club, organization, or sports team. The only difference here was that these were the people who got the better accounts and thus the bigger raises and bonuses. Performance had nothing to do with how much money you made anymore. If you were "in," you were taken care of financially. Furthermore, you couldn't get "in" if you came from meager or average beginnings. I don't know how people found out about others' backgrounds. I mean, we all knew about the ones who bragged about their backgrounds. I guess everyone just deduced that if you didn't brag, you must have nothing since you have nothing to brag about.

I, however, did have something to brag about, but never did. I totally could have played the dad card and secured a permanent position within the popular group, but never wanted to no matter how much I knew I would be accepted. Besides, even if I was "accepted," I'm certain that it would have been with limitations anyway. I was already stooping to so many levels I never thought I would and I just couldn't add to the disappointment in myself. The truth was, my father was a pretty important man. He and a law school friend started their own firm back in the early seventies that has since grown to be one of the largest in New Jersey. Because I never mentioned it, nobody ever assumed I came from wealth. I had a feeling that people were very curious, and I often noticed times where some would try to get information about it out of me. I never caved, though. I think I might have mentioned the word attorney once but never went into detail. That definitely left the others even more curious. I didn't care. I kind of liked having the mystery behind me. I also wanted to move ahead in my professional career on my own merit.

When Todd and his very "hands on" type of management came along, however, that all changed.

First of all, we had to entertain at least two nights a week. There was always some customer in town and we always had to jump at the opportunity to wine and dine him so that not only would his business with us continue, but it would be even more frequent. We had to be the traders he went to for most, if not all, of his business. I can understand and appreciate that, of course, but from my perspective, I saw the cheating, thieving, and lying that went on behind the client's back to get that done. I actually thought at the time that was how every trader at every firm did it. As I was learning more about how this new group was run, I continually asked myself if this was how Roberta would have done it. Part of me just assumed yes. Another cliché I should have listened to at the time, "When you assume, you make an ass out of u and me." I first learned that from my geometry teacher sophomore year of high school. It was true every single time since.

Going out so frequently is tiring in and of itself, but going out with Todd and his entourage was downright exhausting. It wasn't about good conversation, a few cocktails, and a delectable meal. All the fun parts of going out, like I had done with Roberta, totally changed. It was about getting completely annihilated on Cuervo and Patron and staying out so late that you only had enough time to get home, then shower and come right back to work. To these guys, staying out all night and getting a hotel room in the city was the norm. I was not exaggerating when I said that it was a typical high school mentality. I hadn't had to prove to anyone how much I could drink since I was in high school. We were adults here. What was this all about and why was everyone, including myself, following along? We got sucked in, I guess. The powers of Todd were so overwhelming.

A lot of being under Todd's spell had to do with the fact that if you weren't a part of Todd's immediate group, you were nothing to Rich or Clark. Todd only spoke of his intimate crew as being the ones to take notice of and give praise to. Half the time, Todd was feeding his lackeys business or new business ideas and allowing them to pass the business or ideas off as theirs. I'd hear Todd on the phone with one of our clients executing a decent trade and the next day at the morning meeting, one of his "guys" would talk about it as if he himself did it. It was like Todd knew they were a bunch of buffoons and couldn't come up with this stuff on their own. I doubt if Todd even came up with new business ideas on his own. Once, I actually suggested to Todd how to handle a difficult client and he told me that Josh, a loyal follower of his, had already thought of that. Not a minute later I asked Josh about it and Josh had no clue what I was talking about. I mean Todd, come on, if you're going to lie to my face like that, at least cover your tracks. What a moron. Others in the group, who were among the geeks, were outperforming several guys in Todd's entourage, but that didn't matter.

Josh was a very unique individual. He was very arrogant; more arrogant, in fact, than he should have been. He acted a lot smarter than he really was. I remember during one of our morning meetings he was talking about the financial performance of an extremely well-known Fortune 500 company. He said the company's name wrong a few times throughout his speech. Aside from the well-recognized signs all over the country, he should have made sure he knew the name of the place before giving market updates on it and the industry. I was so embarrassed for him. What a boob. He was very cocky overall, even when it came to his looks. For the life of me, I couldn't understand why. It would have been different if he actually tried to look nice, but he didn't. He was a complete slob. He must not have showered regularly. His clothes were always wrinkled, and he had dark red curly hair that looked somewhat clownish. Most times there were fuzzies scattered throughout it because he hadn't even bothered to put a brush through it. He rarely smiled and was a chain smoker. He smelled all the time. He smelled like a combination of stale cigarette smoke and dirty man. And to top it all off, I later found out, he wasn't nice. He just was not a good person. At. All. That's mostly why he seemed so ugly to me. I thought it was odd that Rich even approved of Josh, since Rich was an uptight smug Mr. Perfect. I suppose it was simply because of Josh's arrogance and the fact that he had a penis.

A few months in, Josh began asking me if I wanted to grab lunch with him. This seemed relatively harmless at first, despite the fact that he was in Todd's inner circle. But since he was in that inner circle, I figured I should oblige. Nobody on our desk usually went out to lunch. Most of the time, we'd all just run downstairs to the cafeteria or to one of the many restaurants in the lobby of our building and bring it back to our desks. So basically, I was taking a walk with him downstairs and back to our desks. Eventually, it wasn't harmless anymore. I remember one day when Josh came over to Todd's desk to talk to him about something work related. Josh left, and Todd mentioned that it was clear Josh was smitten with me. Todd then asked me if I would "go for that?" It felt inappropriate and uncomfortable, so I just laughed it off and Todd never brought it up again. Then Josh started asking me out on dates. At first, I would try to reject him as nicely as I possibly could without hurting his feelings. I never wanted to date anyone I worked with, even if he was a nice person, no less someone who was a smelly curmudgeon. Eventually, he got way too persistent. He was pushy and rude about it, in fact. He outright told me that I was making a huge mistake passing up someone like him. I wasn't saying that I was better than he was, just that I was not attracted to him and I worked with him. It was pretty simple. Well, shockingly, he wouldn't take no for an answer, and one night during one of our many post work day outings, things got out of hand. I was sneaking outside of this bar that we usually ended up at late night. I was getting a car back to my apartment, hoping that the guys were all too drunk and too busy patting themselves and each other on the backs to notice me slipping out. Well, Josh happened to notice. I was getting in the car and just as I sat down and was about to close the door behind me, Josh grabbed the door handle and shoved me over to the other side of the seat. (Shit, I was so close!) He was staying at a hotel that night because he was too drunk to travel back to Long Island where he lived. I didn't want to make a big deal about it so, of course, I just kept my mouth shut and let him in. The ride uptown was innocuous, complete with small talk about what a "ragin' good time" that night was. It made more sense geographically to drop me off first and as I was trying to get out of the car, he grabbed my forearm. He was demanding that I go back to his hotel with him. He put his face right up against mine and the stench of beer, tequila, cigarettes, and what could only be described as ass, flooded me.

"Come on, don't get out here. Come with me," he slurred. I think he may have been trying to be all romantic and sexy. Gag.

"No, Josh, I'm home. I'm getting out here."

"Come on, you don't want to go home alone, you want to come with me back to the hotel. I know you do."

"I can't, Josh. Just let me go. Please, I'm tired and really drunk and I need to go." I was still pretty calm at this point. Then he tightened his grip on my arm and pulled it towards him.

"Come on, you're coming with me. Driver, next stop, now!" He was so angry at this point that when he yelled out to the driver saliva came spattering out of his mouth and while most of it ended up on his pants, one drop nestled just above a dried blood crack on the left corner of his lower lip. I couldn't help but notice it. It was so disgusting.

"NO, I'm getting out here!" I'm not even certain if the car was actually at a complete stop as I yanked my arm away from his nicotine stained, mean fingers and bolted out the door, slamming it behind me. I raced up the steps of my apartment as fast as I could for fear of him following me. He didn't. It wasn't long after that my phone was ringing consistently for about ten straight minutes. He ended up leaving me this borderline incoherent voicemail that told me to get over to the hotel where he was stay- ing. (Yeah, okay, I'll be right there.) The next few weeks at work, he was a complete and blatant asshole towards me. If he happened to answer a phone call that turned out to be for me, he'd scream at me in this patronizing voice, like I was his younger sibling, until I picked it up. I never told anyone about what happened, but he was so obviously rude to me that people were asking him what was wrong. I imagined most of them figured out that I rejected his advances. He wasn't too subtle.

Even though Rich didn't partake in the aforementioned nights of gluttony, he knew damn well what went on for the most part. It was up to him to keep it from Clark. And he hid it very well. Rich had to cover for Todd at several big-wig manager morning meetings. I only knew this because, of course, I had to be there to record minutes. Clark's assistant couldn't do it since her delicate little self didn't arrive every morning until eight thirty and these meetings were usually held at seven. I, ever so prompt, always showed up by six thirty, no matter what. Way for that to come back and bite me in the ass, huh? Whenever Todd's sorry, hung-over ass couldn't make it in on time, Richard told Clark and any other authoritative men attending these meetings that he had sent Todd to midtown for a client breakfast or something to that effect. Really fair. Even more, I had to cover for Todd when his wife called in the morning asking for him. I assumed those were the nights that he stayed in a hotel doing God knows what. I was dragging my tired, booze-soaked body to work on time. Todd, and even some of his followers, would stroll in at whatever time they felt like. Todd would often look over at me and smile, "Great time last night, huh?" I would usually just nod and smirk because his behavior literally left me speechless. Besides, if I had opened my mouth any time before eleven a.m. if not to slurp down one of my morning caffeine aids, I was in major fear of vomiting tequila and bar nuts all over my desk.

There were so many times I didn't even want to go out to entertain clients. But Todd insisted that I was not going to get anywhere in this business if I didn't go the extra mile. Entertaining clients was part of the job and I should be honored that I was even asked to go. Not everyone got asked. It was like being one of the popular kids getting invited to all the cool parties. I really didn't see the need to do it as often as we were. I mean, seriously, I had a great roommate and a decent place to go home to every night. Just because these guys wanted to avoid their wives and children didn't mean I had to suffer. Wrong again, oh yes it did.

I was only one of three females on our desk at that time. Roberta had gone to Chicago and another woman was one of the two traders who was laid off right when Clark took over our division. I didn't really know the other women very well. It was strange to me. They would barely give me the time of day. I tried so hard to be nice to them, but they wanted nothing to do with me. This was from when I first started on the desk with Roberta. She told me not to worry about it when she noticed me trying to strike up conversations with them. She said that they've always been like that, even to her, and to not take it personally. I was disappointed at first, but then felt better that I had Roberta. Then when she left, I was disappointed all over again. I didn't feel like there was any sort of camaraderie among the few of us women who were there. There were other women on the trading floor in different departments, trading different products, and none of them were overly friendly. I'd say hello to many of them in the bathroom and most of the time, they'd just give me a once over and look down their noses at me and sputter out a breathy, "Hi."

But even more than the women's treatment, I hated how the guys acted. I hated how they made me feel. All of this behavior was spilling over into the work day, which made everything much worse. Throughout the day, the guys would gather around Todd's desk and sometimes talk business but oftentimes I'd overhear snippets of stories about women they'd hooked up with the previous night. I'd hear details that I didn't care to hear but they didn't care if I'd heard them. The outsiders, or the geeks, could only imagine what it was like on these nights out. They were never asked to join. I would have traded places with any one of them in a heartbeat.

Nights out got so bad that it wasn't just that I didn't want to go anymore, I truly dreaded going. Eventually, I started to learn that there was only one reason I was ever asked to join. I was usually one of only two or three women there unless the guys picked up some Wall Street groupies along the way. Our nights always started out at this bar downstairs in our building. It was a popular hang-out for all of the area's financial companies' workers. Thursdays were the biggest nights out. Wall Street groupies were women who obviously did not work on Wall Street but would get all dolled up to come to this bar or any of the bars nearby to try and land a Wall Street guy. They were usually in fancy revealing dresses with fresh hair and make-up, not like they'd just come off of a full work day on the trading floor.

But I made Todd look cool to his clients in a way the groupies could not. He had this hot young "girl" working for him who did everything he asked, from getting rounds of drinks for everyone to calling the car service for him at four o'clock in the morning to take him home. I was basically his bitch. I really was. I truly thought I was a part of the "in" crowd based on merit. I had the ridiculous notion at first that they all saw me as their equal. I thought I was making strides to help better my career. I wasn't. I was there for Todd to have something to grab or to be pimped out to horny men, who were technically old enough to be my father, looking for someone to fill their king size beds at the Ritz. Even when I tried to talk business with these clients, Todd would swoop in and completely undermine me. Oftentimes, I didn't even see it coming. Eventually, I just let it happen. I figured it was better to be in and be arm candy than to not be in at all.

It had been just about a year since Clark and crew came on board and I was so very ready to jump ship. I was being humiliated on a regular basis. I was repeatedly subjected to verbal and physical sexual abuse in and out of the office setting. It wasn't inconceivable to hear Todd tell me gross things like, "Isn't that shirt a little too loose?" Or "Don't you have too many buttons buttoned?" He would often tell me to go get him something from the printer at the end of our row and there wouldn't be anything there. He said that he just wanted to watch me walk away. I usually just laughed an uncomfortable laugh and pretended like I wasn't offended. I allowed this treatment of me to happen and it continued for a long while. But I was determined to prove that I deserved to be there just as much as those other guys. Soon enough, though, Todd made it very clear to me that my duties did not include managing any accounts and that I was there to do what he told me to do. He never actually said the word "assistant," but that is exactly what I was. I was actually moving backwards in my career. I started off proving myself to be a brilliant trader. My account book for the first three quarters of the year reflected that. But that list of accounts was no longer my list. Todd got all the credit for the business I did and then just picked up where he forced me to leave off. What could I do? He was my boss. He decided how much money I made and could decide to fire me at any time. If I didn't allow him to take advantage of me in every way he did, where would I have ended up? I felt like there was no way out. I had gotten myself into this mess but couldn't figure out a way to get myself out of it.

The announcement of our bonuses almost put me over the edge. After that, instead of the normal continuous denial I was in, I at least progressed by telling myself that eventually, I had to do something about what was going on. I mean, sometime soon in the near future I would tell someone. Yes, I would do it. I would definitely tell somebody; just not yet...very soon though. Maybe I could talk to Jill or to my sister about it. Maybe I could even call Roberta and ask her what I should do. Believe me, that was a huge step for me. At least I admitted to myself that there was a problem and that something needed to be done about it. It was so out of control.

I know it would have seemed like the right time for me to perfect my resume and send it out to other companies. But I had been working at a company that I used to only dream of being at. I knew I'd be the envy of all my college competitors. It was still exciting to be in the hub of the financial industry. Despite how miserable I was, I regularly got goosebumps on certain days when I walked into our building on any given morning because I still couldn't believe I was working at BSJ & Co. I had been there for several years and accrued over a month's worth of personal and vacation days per year. I earned a VP title that Roberta felt I deserved. I had a generous bonus and ample salary to go along with that title. I wasn't ready to give up on BSJ. I still felt an odd sense of loyalty toward it.

So, you see, there was still a glimmer of hope for me. Until bonus day. Richard and Todd met with everyone individually to give us our bonus numbers. We had had a decent year in profits, not the best, but good enough to keep most everyone basically satisfied. Or so I thought. As I watched every person coming out of the conference room there was a pattern. The members of the "in" crew were all smiles. The ones who had the important fathers, who hung out with Todd getting wasted until all hours of the morning, who kept his vicious secrets to themselves, were the ones emerging from that conference room high-fiving each other. The diligent, smart, equally if not more talented guys who were among the unpopular crowd were in sheer shock. They all walked out with the most gruesome looks of disappointment. I was confused. Why such diverse feelings among our group? My confusion dissipated immediately when it was my turn to meet with Rich and Todd. Rich looked me square in the eye and said, "You really didn't bring in any money, so we can't reward you."

Oh Rich. There was so much to tell about Rich. There was so much to hate about Rich. Rich was a first-class jerk. He was a tiny pipsqueak of a man with a huge ego. Can we say Napoleon complex? He was a small, small man on so many levels. He was absolutely the most arrogant person I had ever met. He was a snob. But not a snob in denial like most of the other idiots I worked with. He was a snob and very proud of it. He made it very clear to anyone who encountered him that he considered himself a more significant life form. Everyone hated him; only most of us never admitted it out loud. There was absolutely nothing to like about the guy. But, we all kissed his butt. He probably got off on knowing how dreadful he was to all of us. Well, all of us except Todd. Speaking of which, I never understood Rich's affinity for Todd. At their former company, Todd must've walked on water or something like that. I had absolutely no idea what it could have been. Todd was far from a genius and barely had common sense, for that matter. Todd did seem a bit smarter than the other followers of his but not quite in a business sense. I imagine it was because he had the people skills that Rich lacked so together; they made the perfect team. I digress, I'm sorry. Anyway, Rich was very smug and uptight. He had piercing eyes and a long face like a vulture with this horrid pointy, beak-like nose. He had an extremely short buzz cut, again, not unlike a vulture's head, that appeared to have been trimmed at least every two weeks. Since his hair was a super light blonde, he almost appeared bald at first glance. There was never a hair out of place or a button undone. He looked as tightly wound as he actually was. Every time I saw him I had this intense urge to just drop kick him across the trading floor.

Huh. "Okay, but what about all of the other work I have been doing to keep this group functioning like the well-oiled machine that it is?"

"That has all been very helpful," Rich replied, "but since you are not in a profit-making position, I can't give you a profit maker's bonus." He knew exactly what had happened. He knew that Todd had taken over all of my clients and probably agreed with what he did. Hell, it may have even been his idea.

"Okay, I didn't think that passing my clients over to my manager would mean sacrificing my bonus. I knew that towards the end of this year I hadn't been keeping a book, but I thought that I would benefit for helping the greater good of our group. I also assumed that giving up my book would only be temporary until we could hire Todd an assistant." I guess deep down I knew that there was a chance this could happen, but I didn't think that Todd would have the gall to do it to me. I figured that he would still put in a good word and pass along that it was his idea to recreate my position. I mean, no offense to assistants, but I didn't get a business degree, prepare to take the GMATs to apply to business school, and take all these different Series exams to get registered as a trader so that I could take messages and food orders.

"Sorry Elizabeth, but those clients were finding more and more that they really wanted to deal with me." Todd lied. I still spoke with my former clients on occasion and most, if not all of them, constantly asked me when I was going to be trading for them again. Maybe they were just being nice and said all those things because they knew I wasn't going to. Who knew? Apparently, I couldn't trust anyone anymore.

"Oh, okay then." I was sort of blindsided and completely dumbfounded. I thanked them both and walked out. Ha, I thanked THEM! Not only did my bonus not increase from last year, but it was cut by fifty percent. And Todd didn't do a thing about it. I knew that Rich condoned his behavior, but I didn't think either of them would allow this to happen. Between the two of them there wasn't even an inkling of conscience. I never felt so stupid in my entire life. I was a very intelligent person; how could I let this happen to me? What was I thinking?

Chapter 4

The most disappointing factor in all of this was that I allowed it to change me as a person. Throughout this whole debacle that was my so-called career, I began shutting everyone out. Friends outside of my work environment and family were struggling to break through to me. My work friends, including some who I thought were my friends, knew what was going on and knew why I wasn't myself. But nobody could bring themselves to talk about it. Everyone there knew what was going on and that it was wrong. It was like the huge elephant in the room. The only people who openly addressed it with me were two gentlemen, Tim and John. Neither of them was in the "in" crowd but they were both smart, hardworking men. They knew deep down what scum Rich, Todd, and their loyal followers were.

But really, Jill bore the brunt of it. She had to deal with me at my worst. Fortunately for her, she was dating this really nice fellow, Charlie, whom she met through a friend from her work and spent a lot of time at his place. But there was the occasional week where she and I would cross paths at the apartment. "Liz, I haven't been sleeping at Charlie's place all week, but I haven't seen you either."

"Busy week at work," I'd mutter.

"What time are you getting home at night?"

"Don't know."

"Where are you out 'til all hours?"

"Wherever, with work people." The truth was I didn't want Jill to know anything. She would kill me if she knew what was going on, what I let go on at work. I couldn't handle getting reprimanded from her or anyone else for that matter. I didn't want to deal.

Being in a big Italian family, we always had Sunday dinners together. These usually took place at my parents' house. The whole clan, cousins, aunts and uncles, nieces and nephews all got together to rehash their weeks. It was a way to make sure that everyone was able to stay in everyone else's business. It was mostly only my mother's side of the family, since they were the ones we lived so close to. We were close to my dad's side too, just not geographically. These dinners were a ritual that my mom and her sister, Aunt Donna, thought would end once my grandma died, but they never did. Of course, by that time, my mom and Aunt Donna were grandmothers themselves. I guess it must be some unwritten Italian grandmother rule that you have to have your family near you as much as possible and you must shove as much food in your loved ones' faces as you can. The Sunday dinner ritual sounds a little corny, but deep down, we all loved it. You don't see it that much these days. It was nice.

A few random Sunday nights when it would come time for everyone to leave, my mom would notice that I was coming up with every excuse not to leave their house. I'd stay as late as I could to help her clean and straighten up. She needed the help too. With attendance averaging between twelve and fifteen people per week, there was a pretty big mess.

"Is everything okay with you lately, Elizabeth?"

"Fine, Ma."

"Um, I am your mother, I know when things are not right. Now tell me what is wrong."

"Nothing really, Ma, it's just that work has been really crazy lately."

"Crazy how?"

"Crazy busy, that's all."

"Oh, okay, and you're feeling tired? Is that it?"

"Yeah, really tired."

"I can tell. You're looking like you're not getting enough rest."

"Gee, thanks. That's the nice way of saying I look like hell, right?"

"No, tired. Beautiful, but tired nonetheless." Textbook mom response.

The ride back to the city that night was absolute hell. I agonized over not telling her. I wanted to so badly, but saying it out loud would make the pain so real. It would mean that all of those bad things that did happen were really true. I cried so hard I had to pull over. I sat there for about twenty minutes before I could muster up the energy to continue driving. My Sunday blues didn't really ever hit until it was time to go to bed. If I got back to the apartment and Jill wasn't there, they sometimes came a little early. That night, they started the moment my mother asked me if I was okay.

No matter how tired I was, the Sunday blues prohibited me from falling asleep. I would watch a lot of TV and read tons of magazines and trashy romance novels. The TV shows had to be fun, uplifting programs. Sometimes I would scroll through the cable channels and look for a classic comedy. I had to immerse myself in lighthearted entertainment in order to keep the negative horror of the week to come from entering my system. It never really worked, though. I was totally fooling myself. I mean, as funny as Aunt Edna from *National Lampoon's Vacation* was, she was not going to miraculously save me from the torture that was my job. As soon as I turned off the TV or closed the book or magazine, I knew exactly how my next two to three hours were going to be spent. I'd stare at the ceiling of my alcove, if Jill wasn't home, or the ceiling of our living room if she was. I was afraid that my tossing and turning and getting up and down for a glass of water or to go to the bathroom would wake her. It was bad enough that I was walking around like a zombie. I didn't need her to be losing sleep too. This particular night, Jill was there.

"What the hell are you doing?" Jill barked at me. I was on the bathroom floor. I was covered in sweat and my hair was glued to the side of my pale green face.

"Shit. Nothing. Leave me alone, I'm fine."

"Huh, really, you're fine? Well, you certainly don't look fine!" She was on the verge of yelling now.

"Jill, seriously, now is so not the time, okay?"

"No, it is not okay. What is going on?"

"I'm sick."

"Thanks, Captain Obvious. Why? What's wrong?"

"I must've eaten something bad. Sour milk or uncooked meat or something, now can you leave me alone, so I can get this raunchy bacterium out of my system?" She gave me the hairy eyeball. You know that look? The one that says, *I'm on to you. I don't know what you're up to, but I will find out.* It was a half joking, half serious stare. She didn't know whether to strangle me or scoop me up, cradle me like a baby, and hug me. I looked back at her. "Well, can I puke in private?"

"In a sec, flush that. I have to pee."

"K, hurry though." With that she wiped, flushed, and swooped our shower curtain of a door open and closed and went back to bed. I was totally busted. She knew. I mean, she didn't know exactly what was going on, but she knew something that had to do with my job was breaking me. I had mentioned some of my issues with the job to Jill. I didn't get into the ridiculous harassment, but I did tell her about my idiot manager and how he was taking my client book over. She usually just told me to say something directly to him and couldn't understand why I hadn't. It was so much more complicated than that for me. Being upfront for Jill came very easily. She fully respected my privacy that night but knew that it was a matter of time before I crumbled. She gave me my space, but I knew that it wouldn't be long before she would force it out of me if I didn't confide in her soon. The truth was I had been having these panic attacks on a regular basis for quite some time now. I thought one night as I hovered over the toilet that I heard Jill rustling around the apartment. I guess this wasn't the first time she'd found proof that something was up. As the sweat poured down my face and dripped off my nose, I wiped it away. The shakes subsided, and my heart slowed to a normal steady pace. I got up, brushed my teeth, and climbed back into bed. This routine was almost my every Sunday night for the past six months. The entire process usually lasted about two and a half to three hours. I'd finally calm down and drift off to sleep. Depending on what time I actually did fall asleep, I usually got between two and four hours of sleep. Considering the little amount of rest that I got during the week, I should have been banking some major snooze time on Sundays.

The main reason for not telling anyone what was going on at work was because I was ashamed. I was ashamed that I let this happen to me. I hadn't been an angel myself this past year. I got what I deserved. If I had only been a stronger person, I could have stood up to Todd and those other jackass followers of his. There were so many times I could've just gotten mad and fought back or told somebody... anybody. I never did at the time.

Part Two

This Too Shall Pass

Chapter 5

There I was, sitting in my bathtub, hugging my bent knees, fully clothed with the shower running on my back, feeling like my soul had just been ripped out of me. I was trying to replay the events of that evening in my head, figuring out how I had gotten to this point, but so much of it was unclear to me. Calculating the number of drinks I had versus the amount of food I ingested, I realized that I was pretty wasted. Was I so wasted that I could've actually allowed the events that took place to happen? It all felt like some horrific nightmare. I enjoyed the alcoholic beverage on many occasions, but I was always confident in the way that I handled myself when I was drunk. Why was tonight different? Why were so many parts of the night a blur? I couldn't figure it out, so I just kept going over and over in my head what I could remember.

My whole body was shaking. I had been crying so much but there were no more tears and I was left hyperventilating. I couldn't even catch my breath. My head was throbbing. I ran my fingers along my hairline behind my ear. There was a lump the size of a golf ball. Grazing over it with my fingers caused the throbbing to intensify. Son of a bitch that hurt! Casualty. I had almost forgotten about that. I could feel the mascara residue crusting all around my eyes. They were burning. I wanted to rip my contact lenses out in that instant but didn't have the energy. I couldn't move, no less function enough to put anything near my eyes. I saw the hair that was resting on my shoulders was dull and matted. There were so many knots in it and the fact that the water was pouring over most of it didn't help. I was dreading the moment I eventually would have to put a brush through it. I had no idea what time it was, but I knew at least that it was late on a Friday night or early Saturday morning, whichever. Was the sun about to come up? How long had I been sitting here?

It had been our work holiday party that night. I would never have been out with work people otherwise on a week-end night. They didn't earn weekend status. Weekends are what I looked forward to, relaxing, enjoyable times with folks I loved. There was no way I was going to waste precious weekend hours with the morons I was ready to plant six feet under, unless, of course, it was the holiday party.

The invention of the holiday party was as cruel as the invention of panty hose. I mean, who in their right mind thought it would be a good idea to cram dozens of people who actually mostly loathe one another into a small private room at a restaurant and force them to not only socialize but cele-brate what is supposed to be the most joyous time of year? It was completely suffocating, binding, in fact. It was as if some-one was taking said panty hose from around my waist and hoisting them up over my head so that my nose was smashed against my face like a burglar's. I was so annoyed just being there. Nobody wanted to be there, but we all knew that we had to attend. There were rumors that we would get to see Clark in the flesh. Those rumors turned out to be true. The head of our division put on his best pep rally grin for his first official holiday party in his position. People were doing anything to make sure he saw them, including bouncing across his path by parading the bunny hop line right under his nose. Every-one knew that making an appearance at the ridiculous event wouldn't get them a huge promotion, but we all felt the need go and have him see us there nonetheless.

The party itself was completely harmless. I was truly shocked when I got a moment with Clark and he knew me by my first name. Granted, it took me being right at Todd's side to get him to notice me, but being the loyal ass kiss that I was, I wouldn't have been anywhere else at the time. I couldn't just let Todd get his own drinks, now could I? God forbid. Every so often he looked up from his glass and handed me his money clip and gestured towards the bar. No, it wasn't a cash bar. BSJ & Co. was cheap and I wouldn't be surprised if they had done that, but they didn't. I had to keep tipping generously so I wouldn't, I mean Todd wouldn't, have to wait long for his next drink. I was used to waiting on him, though. That was a regular occurrence given the number of times we were in a bar on any given week. He didn't even ask anymore. I was like a trained puppy. I was such an idiot.

It was not even two minutes into my conversation with Clark that someone interrupted us. Todd grabbed me by the arm and told me to round everyone up but to do it nonchalantly. Todd didn't want any of the "losers" finding out where we were going afterwards. I wondered why we were even going anywhere else; there were no clients there. There wasn't a soul around for us to have to entertain. But, as usual, I kept my mouth shut and went along with it. I had no idea where we were going. In fact, I never had any idea where we were going. I knew it had to be some swanky, hard-to-get-into restaurant, followed by some discreet red velvet rope club. The wee hours of the morning were often-times very predictable. I gathered that wherever we went after the holiday party, by the tail end of the night, we'd be at our usual spot. By two thirty or so most nights out, we were routinely stumbling into Sami MacIlstout's. It was a decent bar, but I absolutely hated going there. I imagined that Sami's could have been fun had I gone with people I truly liked. It was one of those places where girls always got up on top of the bar during the cheesiest songs and danced for the crowd. Oftentimes they got rather salacious, but that was always encouraged, especially by the walking hormones I was with.

The water that was beating down on me from the shower was ice cold and it took me a while to realize it. I was numb. I was thinking about how differently the night would have turned out had I just come home after the party. I was banging my head against the tile along the side of our shower as if to knock some sense into myself. What was wrong with me? Up until then, I'd never felt so miserable or so disappointed in myself. I finally stood up and stripped. I left my clothes in a sloppy soggy pile at the bottom of our tub. I climbed out, soaking wet, and turned the faucet off. It was then that the cold really hit me. Now I was trembling from the chill too. I shuffled over to our makeshift linen closet, three white crates erected right outside the so-called bathroom door, and grabbed a towel. Thank God Jill was at her boyfriend's place. I was glad that she had been spending so much time there lately. She was happy. He was a great guy. She didn't need to be around me. I was a drag. I couldn't cover up how frustrated I was anymore, and that night was the final straw. I just didn't even know where to begin from there. I checked the time; it was 5:46 AM. Great, knowing I wasn't going to get a decent night's sleep stressed me out a little bit. I felt like I needed a clear head so I could figure out what I was going to do about this work situation. Since our heater never seemed to work, I always had three different blankets on my bed. I climbed in without even taking the towel off and putting my pajamas on, and wrapped myself up, head included. Although I knew it was practically impossible, I hoped to be able to at least get a solid six hours. I wanted nothing to do with anyone or anything outside my little cocoon of a bed, at least for that one night.

I was very restless throughout the early morning hours that Saturday. I must've gotten out of bed a hundred times thinking I was going to puke or needing a glass of water. I eventually changed from the wet towel, but my hair was still damp when I tried to get out of bed around eleven thirty. I got as far as my couch and collapsed there. I took my favorite blanket from my bed with me. I got this blanket as part of a housewarming gift from my folks. My sister so appropriately named it the Amazing TV Suit. It was incredibly warm. It had a black watch plaid flannel pattern on one side and had this soft insulation on the other. Why a suit? Well, it had these snaps up the side so when you wrapped it around you, you could snap it closed. It also rested ever so neatly around your neck and snapped closed at your chest with these two holes for your hands to stick out. These holes allowed for simple maneuvering of such things like the remote control, a book, or even a plate of food. You could move about and never get cold because the blanket couldn't fall off. The bottom could have been closed when you were lying down, or you could have left it open for your feet to stick out if you needed to get across the apartment. I looked like a monk when it was all snapped up, but I never cared. It was warm. It was awesome. My mother was so excited when she gave it to me. "You could wear it while you're watching TV!" And so the Amazing TV Suit was born. Little did either of us know what an important "companion" this suit would be to me.

My phone rang. I didn't even flinch. I had no desire to talk to anyone. I knew that if I had, I'd just start blubbering and wouldn't be able to hide my misery. That's all I wanted to do. Hide my misery. I wasn't ever supposed to be miserable. I was Elizabeth. Everyone knew me as the happy, optimistic one. I didn't want anyone in my family to know that I wasn't in good shape, especially my parents or Heather. I didn't want anyone worrying. I was nervous about Jill finding out, but grateful I could prolong that, thanks to her love life. I was just sitting on the couch wrapped up in the Amazing TV Suit like a burrito. I couldn't collect my thoughts. My mind was all over the map. I was reflecting on the past year at that job and couldn't fathom how I had gotten to where I was. Ugh. Where was I to start? I decided that the first thing to do was to focus on how I was going to deal with Todd on Monday morning.

He had been a severe jerk to me and was especially brutal last night. Throughout that day, the events from the prior evening were coming back to me in dribs and drabs. I couldn't believe that I didn't even have the courage to stand up for myself. Eventually, I was going to maybe contact Human Resources or possibly bring up my issues with everything, particularly Todd and Josh, to Clark. But how would I even get an appointment with Clark? I wasn't sure, but I had a couple of days to figure it out. The main fear I had to conquer was Todd. All I could do was prepare myself with different responses to different things he could say to me. I actually wrote them down and rehearsed them. I tried every scenario I could think of. He could be very apologetic and ask for my forgiveness. He could be arrogant and blame the whole ridiculously awful night on me. I wasn't sure, but I wanted to be ready to deal with him.

By the end of the day, I felt okay. I had to convince myself that standing up to him no matter what he said to me was the right thing to do. Everything had gone too far. Every little prick in his entourage thought that they, too, could treat me like crap, the way Todd did. I had enough. Things were completely out of hand and they would only get worse. I continued to talk myself up. I gave myself a pep talk. I had an answer for everything he could possibly throw my way. Phew, I was pleased with myself. As exhausting as it was, I was proud to at least have my wits about me to organize my plan. I then relaxed a little.

It was a Saturday night and I was not in any mood to be social. I didn't answer any of my friends' phone calls. The high school gang was all going to be out in Hoboken and wanted me to join them. Brian was bringing his fiancée, Susan. I really wanted to get to know her better, but I just wasn't up to it. I had more important things to fix in my life. So, I lied. I said I was sick. Lying to people and avoiding them is much easier than lying to their faces. I had a stomach flu. That's the best illness to lie about having because nobody can call you out for not sounding sick. That was also what I told my mother when I called the next morning to say that I wouldn't be making it to Sunday dinner. I just couldn't bear to go. I actually really wanted to go but knew I would completely break down if I did. It was hard leaving there on Sundays as it was, but after the few days I had had, there was no way I could go and keep every horrid, gut-wrenching feeling inside.

"Hey Ma, what are you doing?"

"Oh, just making the meatballs for this afternoon. Daddy and I went to ten thirty mass instead of noon so I could get a head start on dinner. What time are you heading over?"

"Actually, that's why I'm calling. I'm not going to come today."

"Oh, how come, you okay?"

"No, I am really sick... stomach flu. I haven't been able to keep anything down since yesterday morning." Lie.

"Did you take anything?"

"No, if it's a bug I'd rather just let it escape my system." Damn, not bad for thinking on my toes.

"Do you have a fever?"

"Nope, not today, I might've yesterday though. Ma, I'm fine, Jill's boyfriend had it earlier in the week and I must've gotten it from him." Another lie.

"Are you drinking lots of water? You have to make sure that you replenish your system so you don't get dehydrated."

"Uh huh, yes, Mother."

"Alright then, you get your rest. I'll check back with you tonight."

Awesome. Lying to my mother. That felt great. I knew that I just had to get through the next couple of days. I would stand up to Todd and depending on how he took it, I'd file an official complaint so he could never do anything like that to me or anyone else again. Then I could talk about it with my mom, my sister, or Jill. The phone rang. Caller ID, Godsend, might actually be even better than sliced bread. It was my sister.

"Hello Heather, what's up?" I tried to sound a little under the weather, however that might sound, because I knew that she just spoke with my mother and my mother told her that I wasn't coming.

"You better not be hungover. Are you hungover?"

"No, I'm not hungover, I am legitimately sick, I swear."

"You know it's paint and wallpaper Sunday, Elizabeth. You can't bail on me!' Heather was half joking and half furious. "You know I'm not good at deciding this stuff. Mom is renovating the *entire* upstairs and you're leaving the decisions on what she should do with the walls up to me? She's only narrowed her choices down to like seventy-five colors and patterns! I can't help her choose with that many options!"

"I know. I'm sorry. I was so sick yesterday that if I wasn't either on the toilet or kneeling in front of it, I was sleeping. Besides, it's not seventy-five!"

"It seems like it. Ugh, I could kill you."

"Oh, come on, suck it up. It's not that bad. You guys will manage just fine without me. I'm not the only one with good decorating taste. I may be more decisive than you both but that's all. You'll figure it out."

"Okay, feel better. Call me during the week. Talk to you later."

Heather and I usually chatted at least twice a week. She was married with two kids, Thomas and Edward. She had a great family. Keith, her husband, was a terrific husband and father. I was always so happy that Heather and I were close. Oftentimes I thought of her as a third parent. She was very much the older sister and I was very much the younger sister. We meshed well. When I hung up the phone with her, I returned to my couch with the Amazing TV Suit and was a bum all day. It was quite nice, actually. It was a good way to rest up and prepare for my big day.

Chapter 6

O nce again, sleep was scarce that Sunday night. I never slept well on Sundays as it was, but that time was even worse. I was extraordinarily anxious. I was anticipating what was going to happen when I arrived at work. I actually woke up about a half an hour before my alarm went off and decided just to get up and start getting ready. After my shower, I stretched up on my tiptoes to get a closer look in the mirror and inspected the lump behind my ear. Good, it was hidden by my hair, nothing to worry about. I was ready to walk out the door when I took a deep breath, closed my eyes and told myself that everything was going to be alright. I couldn't believe I was running off a cliché to myself. Was I lying to myself? Was it really going to be okay? I didn't know that for a fact, who was I kidding? At the time, I believed it. I needed to believe it.

The subway ride downtown that morning seemed like an eternity. At least I was sitting down. Seats were plentiful at six o'-clock in the morning. The one good thing about my commute was that it was early enough to be before heavy rush hour, so it was much less frustrating. I was bundled in my winter garb and it was exceptionally hot in the car. My palms had already been sweating due to nerves. It got so bad that my fingertips were ac-tually pruning. I took my mittens off and blew on my hands. Yes, I wore mittens. They're so much warmer than gloves. I swore by them. The guy standing almost directly in front of me looked up from his *Wall Street Journal* the instant I put both hands up to my face. He chuckled, gave me a little grin and returned to his paper. I usually read during my ride, too, but couldn't focus that morning. I had my paper rolled up in my bag, figuring I'd possibly get to it at a later point during the day. Believe it or not, that stranger laughing at the goofball I was, relieved me a little bit; even if it was only for a few seconds. Hey, I took what I could get.

None of Todd's followers knew what went on with him and me Friday night. Usually their Monday morning conversations would revolve around some feat that Todd just had to brag about. They were never discreet with one another about being egotistical womanizing scum. Todd was exceptionally close with Josh and I thought for a while that he might've told Josh, but he hadn't. I didn't think that Todd would talk about what he had done to me with anyone. He couldn't have been that dumb. He trusted Josh a lot though. He'd have Josh "cover for him" if his wife called on a day that Todd never made it home the prior night. Those were the really bad nights when some of them partied so much that they all ended up staying at a hotel. It happened more than I probably even knew. Most of the time on those kinds of nights, I was able to escape the zoo. I could slither out of Sami MacIl-stout's quietly enough so as not to disturb the drunken animals. Sometimes, I even got away. Other times Todd, the zookeeper, would lasso me in and attach a leash to my neck to make sure I couldn't disappear from his sight. On the rare occasion, I was permitted to go home after work. My boss had actually said to me once, "You're off the hook. It's a 'no bitches allowed' night." They were all pigs and I could see them in a sick, twisted way bragging about belittling women, but nothing happened that morning to suggest Todd said anything to anyone. That was the only good thing.

Since I was always just about the first person to show up, I had a few minutes to settle myself in. I got my cup of coffee, turned on my computer and pulled out my paper. I tried to read it but found myself just staring at the front page. I was thinking of a million different other things. I usually spent this time every morning to prepare for my day. I was pretty anal retentive about planning. I was organized as hell and very neat. My desk was impeccable at all times and I could always find what I was looking for. Annoying as it seemed, it kept my mind tidy and together if my stuff was tidy and together. One time, I'll never forget, Roberta took advantage of my neatness compulsion and played a subtle but hysterical joke on me. She used to constantly ask me why every pile of papers, my calendar, my stapler, my rolodex, my trade blotter and my notebook all had to be laid across my desk at ninety-degree angles. I could never give her an answer better than, "Because, that's how I like it." So, she took it upon herself one day when I was out to move everything, ever so slightly, off the right angle. Things were moved about five degrees in either direction, so that when I returned the next morning, I'd find my desk in what I considered total disarray. Mind you, we only had about three feet of desk space each, so I thought my anal retentiveness was a necessity. Everyone on our desk was in on it, so you can imagine the grief I got. I thought that was some pretty clever stuff. It hurt to think back to the Roberta days.

As more and more people started to arrive, the level of noise on the trading floor increased. It was like I could tell what time it was without even looking at the clock. Every morning was the same routine. Each person showed up the same time every day. We were like programmed robots. When it sounded as if it was approaching seven, I knew that Todd would be in soon. It was a Monday, so he usually was on time on Mondays. I guess that's because there were never any client dinners on Sundays. Well, never say never, right? I thought I had enough time to run to the ladies' room and either flush myself down a toilet or splash my face with some cold water. I chose the latter. But there he was in the faint distance getting closer. He was actually a little early. "Strange," I mumbled to myself. He was never early. Maybe he wanted to take some extra time to talk with me. I felt my heart's thick heavy beat with each step he took. Thump, thump, thump... gulp. He had this haughty stride. He was so conceited the way he swung his arms and held his head as he strutted down the hall and onto the trading floor. It used to be mildly intimidating. It wasn't anymore. It was nauseating. I wanted to roll my eyes at him as he approached me, but what I thought about him and how I acted towards him were two different things. I was such a hypocrite. He breezed by me without so much as a glimpse and plopped his royal ass down in his chair next to mine. He sputtered a, "Morning" to me and got on the phone almost instantly. Actually, it wasn't even to me, it was at me; he didn't even look in my direction. He spoke straight ahead as if he was greeting his computer screen. He was being a jerk and I was prepared for that, somewhat.

The entire morning was mostly that ridiculously immature behavior from him. He'd mix it up with a little business talk but for the most part couldn't look me in the eye. Good, the bastard was sorry for what he did to me, he felt guilty. He was bound to say something to me by the end of the day. The day carried on.

Huh, four thirty and not a peep about Friday night. A few folks were recapping the party and he chimed in, but that was it. Five thirty came and went and now it was almost six. I noticed that he was closing down his computer. Okay, he was probably waiting until the end of the day right before he left to talk to me, that way he didn't have to sit next to me for hours feeling ashamed. He rolled his chair back to the closet between the window panes and grabbed his coat. He stood up, threw it over his shoulders, and shoved his arms through, all in one swift motion. As he walked by my desk behind me, he placed his hand on me where the top of my shoulder meets my neck and said, "Don't work too hard. G'night." As he lifted his hand off me, the back of it brushed against my neck and then my cheek. I got the chills, but not in a good way. It was creepy. The hairs on the back of my neck stood up. I didn't even look at him. Wow, was he not going to bring it up at all? He couldn't. I did not plan for that! I hadn't run through that scenario. I didn't even think about what to do if I had to say something first. He should have to, he was the boss. He had the power. I didn't. I should have just popped out of my seat then and there and told him off, but I never did. Why was he doing this to me?

The next few days Todd didn't prove to grow a conscience. Still nothing. He acted as if Friday never happened. I found it very bizarre. How could this guy completely take advantage of me on so many levels and not be decent enough to take responsibility for his actions? Was I overreacting? Had I deserved to be taken advantage of and humiliated? Fortunately, throughout the week, I was sidetracked a little bit because the mood around the trading floor was very positive. It was late December, everyone was cheerful. Business was always light this time of year. There were some days people even left early because there wasn't too much going on. It was a nice time for them to get some of their Christmas shopping done, I guess. It had been a week since the holiday party and I hadn't even made plans for the upcoming weekend. I had a few parties I could have gone to, but I didn't really feel like it. I was sad. Work officially got to me.

The next week was very lackadaisical. Christmas was on a Wednesday and some kids had off from school a full two weeks. Some of my colleagues would bring their children into work with them. There was an annual party for the kids held in our cafeteria. It was cute. Santa and his elves were there, and the children ate lunch and got all kinds of goodies. Even the older kids, who were above all that, came in. They just liked playing on the computers and hanging out. I'll never forget that Christmas Eve when Todd's family paid him a nice little visit.

Todd walked up to me, wife and baby in tow, with another little one tugging at her pants, and introduced me to her. "Elizabeth, this is Sylvia." What a sleaze. I wish I just came right out and told her that she was married to a complete jackass, but of course, I didn't. I couldn't. That would have just been stupid.

Instead, I eloquently said "It's a pleasure to finally meet you in person. We've spoken over the phone so many times. It's nice to put a face with a name." She and I examined each other. I think she was taken aback by my looks. I got the impression that she hadn't imagined me to be at all attractive. She looked at me as if to say, *You are young, you are pretty, and I hate that you spend so much time with my husband.*

"Likewise," she replied gracefully. I sensed that she had minimal trust in Todd. She was no fool. I couldn't even begin to comprehend why Todd would not want to rush home to her every night. She was drop dead gorgeous. She was tall, model tall, and had perfect blonde shoulder length hair cut in the trendiest style. Her eyes were a fierce blue and her facial features were perfect. Had she been to a plastic surgeon? Possibly. Her flawless skin radiated and despite the fact that she had a child about nine months prior, her body was excessively thin. Her casual attire screamed designer expensive. Her jeans and cream-colored turtleneck sweater probably cost more than my college education. Sylvia's overall look was polished off with a rock the size of Rhode Island on her perfectly manicured finger. That and the wedding band combined must've totaled about eight carats. The set was bigger than her hand. It looked as if her gaunt little finger was going to snap off. Either that or her bone thin arm was suffering tremendous muscle strain from holding it up. I told myself that it was okay to be overly critical, since I knew she was doing the same to me. I felt her eyes penetrate every inch of my body. I couldn't help but believe that I was the enemy for a moment there. It was incredibly uncomfortable. We made small talk for a few minutes. I would rather have been hung from the ceiling by my eyelids. It would've been less painful. Luckily three phone lines started ringing at once and I had to excuse myself from the awkwardly painful situation.

"Nice meeting you, Sylvia. Merry Christmas."

"Same to you, Elizabeth." And with her fake smile, she was just as relieved as I was to terminate that debacle of a conversation. I watched as she made her way around to Todd's cohorts. I sat back down in my chair and thanked God that it was Christmas Eve and that the day was a short one. When I checked the time, I noticed that it was almost noon. Itching to free myself from the hell that was my job, I started logging off my computers. I didn't know for sure if it was okay to leave for the day, nor did I care. I was so annoyed that I couldn't stay there for another minute. I gathered my stuff and left abruptly. I didn't think twice about it and never looked back. I felt like I was going to burst if I didn't leave right then and there. I didn't say goodbye to anyone or wish anyone a Merry Christmas. I ran for the elevator and willed it to descend faster. By the time I got outside I was almost in a full-blown panic attack. The brisk December air hit me like a ton of bricks and I managed to catch my breath. I got back to my apartment in one piece and finished packing up my bag for the long weekend. I had taken the Thursday and Friday after Christmas off and I was looking forward to being home.

Chapter 7

My apartment was empty as usual, so I managed to pack quickly and hit the road. I had sent an email to Jill earlier in the week to see if she wanted a ride back home but she replied that she and Charlie both had Christmas Eve off and since he had a car, she'd go with him. I hadn't even realized that they had gotten serious enough to celebrate Christmas together. What was wrong with me? What kind of friend was I? The truth was I missed her. She and I hadn't spent that much time together the past few months with her being at Charlie's place all the time and with me being so wrapped up in work. I knew I had to make the extra effort to hang out with her at some point this weekend. Her family usually came over to our house for dessert on Christmas Eve, so I figured we'd plan some quality time then. Since I had left work so early, traffic wasn't too bad getting out of the city. I made it to my parents' house a lot more quickly than I thought I would. I was in a daze the entire ride though. I was thinking about work, Jill, my high school friends and very much looking forward to seeing my family. I needed to be home. It was my safety zone.

No matter where I hung my hat, the house I grew up in was always considered home for me. My apartment was my apartment, but my parents' house was home. I always felt this overwhelming feeling of warmth upon entering. It was such a powerful feeling. Too strong to even put into words. It was like being wrapped up in the best hug imaginable. Christmas was especially welcoming. My mother was a decorating fanatic. The house was trimmed to perfection. It was like something out of a catalogue. The tree was flawless as if it was on display in a window at Macy's. Every single bulb was perfectly placed. All of the balls and bows were color coordinated and evenly distributed. Every archway in the house was donned with greenery and lights; and not one electrical cord in plain sight, ever. Everything in that house during the month of December was changed over for the holiday season. Each trinket on display on every shelf was a snowman or a Santa statue or something of the like. Curtains in the kitchen, hand towels in the bathrooms, and even throw rugs transformed to create this lavish wonderland. It's amazing how she had the patience to do it every year. Actually, my father got credit for a lot of it too. He barely had time to digest his Thanksgiving Day turkey before he'd be in the crawlspace and up in the attic retrieving these boxes of joy. He'd grunt and groan and take orders from my mom about how every little detail had to be perfect. In the end though, I'd say it was all worth it. It's still up in the air whether he agrees.

Christmas Eve was my favorite day of the year; and no, not only because of the food, although that did have a lot to do with it. It was always the biggest holiday in my family and thus a major production. As soon as I opened the door, I got a waft of the long awaited all too familiar smell of the lobster sauce. It was tradition that both my grandmothers carried over from Italy to have fish on Christmas Eve. The first course was usually shrimp cocktail, fried shrimp (insert Forrest Gump's Bubba voice here), stuffed baked clams, and mussels. Then we'd have this cod fish salad called bacalao, which very few of us ever ate. The last course was the linguine with lobster tails and fillet. My olfactory senses were in overdrive.

My sister, her two boys, and my aunt were already there. I arrived right in the middle of everyone which was perfect, because I got the instant gratification from my nephews but not the overload from everyone all at once. It was funny to think how we all spent most Sundays together yet on Christmas Eve we acted like we hadn't seen each other in years. Soon enough, the house was busting at the seams with boisterous laughter, full bellies, and shreds of wrapping paper. For the first time in my life, I didn't care to participate. I thought that just being at home would lift my spirits, but it didn't. I barely ate and was relatively quiet compared to my usual garrulous self. I had to disappear every so often up to my old bedroom so I could go cry. I couldn't hold it inside. I couldn't fight it. It wasn't like a lump in my throat or a little tear in my eye, it was full-fledged crying. I was defenseless against it. It was uncontrollable at times. I thought I was being artfully stealth until my mother mentioned something to me.

It was approaching three thirty in the morning and the house was finally calm. I was in my bathroom taking out my contacts and my dad was asleep when my mother called up to me from the foyer. "Elizabeth, come down here and help me polish off this bottle of wine. I'd hate to waste it." I accepted that challenge.

"Be right down." I finished preparing for bed and slowly made my way back down to the living room. There were remnants of the evening all over the place. The lights were dim and the deep red embers in the fireplace were glowing. The piles of opened gifts were neatly stacked under the tree. The washer and dryer were rhythmically humming and hard at work cleansing the linens for Christmas Day dinner. I plopped my butt on the chair opposite my mother, threw a blanket over my legs and she poured me the last few drops of wine.

"So..." she inquired.

"So?" I looked over at her and she gave me quite an intense glare. It was a glare that only a mother could give. It was the one that said, *Enough is enough. You're not okay. Do not insult my intelligence. Tell me what is going on.*

"Listen, I'm not trying to pry or get you upset or angry with me. But enough is enough. You're not okay. Do not insult my intelligence. Tell me what is going on with you." See, I knew it. I paused for a moment and took a few deep breaths. I had to buy some time while I tried to concoct some lavish lie about how I was dating a guy who just completely broke my heart or something like that. Then I realized that I pretty much shared everything with her and my sister and if I were involved with someone they'd both know about it. I quickly tried to come up with something else. I thought that maybe I could say something bad about work but not get into full detail. I thought that I could tell her that I was fighting with Jill. I thought and thought and thought about telling her all these different things, but I never thought of telling her the truth. I didn't have to. I exploded into tears. I hated that feeling of being okay until someone asked me if I was okay. Then I'd go and release everything I'd been trying to hold in all at once. That was basically what happened.

"I can't, I can't, I just can't..." I sputtered between snorts. "I don't want to talk now. I can't. I will, I promise, but not now. I don't know." She comforted me like nobody ever could without even saying a word. "I'm a mess. I am all off. I am stupid, I've done stupid things. I am a disaster. Just don't ask me about it yet. Not yet." I had no idea when or how I was going to tell her. I begged her not to mention anything to anyone, not even my father or Heather. She reluctantly agreed.

"I promise I won't tell anyone, but you're not doing as good a job of hiding it as you think. Heather mentioned something to me while we were cleaning off the table tonight."

"What did you say?"

"I told her that I had no idea what was bothering you. I told her the truth."

"I'm sorry. You shouldn't have to answer for me. I've been avoiding any sort of intimate conversation with her to avoid her catching on."

"Just tell me one thing and I won't ask you another question about it until you are ready to talk to me."

"What?"

"Are you sick?"

"No Ma, I swear it is nothing like that."

Christmas Day came and went, and the rest of the weekend was rather awkward, because I felt like my mother was just waiting for me to spill my guts to her. I knew she was anxious, but she kept her promise by not telling anyone about my breakdown. I have to admit, I felt a little relieved afterward. The extreme crying coupled with her silent compassion was quite cathartic. I was able to get out and actually meet up with some of my high school friends that Friday and Saturday night. On Friday night it was just Kristin, Marissa, and me; girls' night. We went to dinner and caught up with one another. I filled the girls in with the slightest bit of detail about how my job was really stressful and that I was thinking of changing. I was extremely vague but emphasized how nice it was and how much I needed to be with them. Neither of them pressed the issue any further.

On Saturday, Steve, Jim, Brian, and Brian's fiancée Susan met up with us. I was able to keep my mind off of things enough to enjoy myself again. Holiday weekends were big nights to go out back home. It was as if there was a phone chain and everyone from my class and the year ahead of us found out where people were going to meet up. Not everyone from both graduating classes went out, of course, but enough of us did to consider these events spontaneous mini reunions. I was very nervous at first but was relieved to find myself having a great time. When other people besides my close friends asked what I was up to, I told them that I lived in the city and lied that I loved my job. I managed. And after a few glasses of wine, it all got easier. My cousin, who had been going through a divorce at the time, came with me that Saturday night since it was a bigger group of people. He has a son who, at the time, was about five years old. It wasn't an easy divorce, so I invited him out with hopes of him letting loose and having a good time despite the trouble he was going through. It felt good to be around someone else whose world was falling apart. He came. It was hilarious when my friend, Brian, ordered

71

a round of shots for everyone and my cousin said that he couldn't do one because he had to get up early to take his son ice skating the next day. It was a big adventure for them. They were going to the tree at Rockefeller Center and spending the day in the city. My cousin didn't want to be hungover or dragging. It made sense. Well, Brian would have none of it! He told my cousin, "Of all the excuses I've heard people say when they don't want to do a shot, that is, by far, the lamest!" With that, Brian handed all of us the shots and we cheered to the holidays and good friends and my cousin did the shot with us. He ended up being totally fine the next day, but he didn't hear the end of it that entire night. It was such a great night out. My life may have seemed like a disaster because of work, but thanks to my amazing friends and family, I did manage to have some wonderful times despite it all.

At the end of the night on Saturday, the group of us took a cab back to Marissa's folks' house. It was the closest place to the bar where all of us could crash for the night. I woke up really early and Marissa's dad was kind enough to drop my hungover ass off at my car. I reflected as I drove back home on how happy I was to have enjoyed myself. It had been such a long time that I felt that way.

I was completely thrilled for my friend Brian. He and Susan seemed very happy. It was like they were meant for each other. I gave Susan credit for cracking into our little circle. We were a pretty tight group and were not about to just welcome anyone into it. Well, our barks were worse than our bites. If Brian loved her, we knew we'd love her. I loved my friends so much. I was so lucky to have them in my life. Jim was the clown of the group, and Steve was the smart, levelheaded one. I felt a stronger connection with Steve over the other guys. I don't know why exactly. We were the opposite-sex pair that grew close among our group without ever hooking up or dating. There might have been some light incestuous make out sessions among the larger group of us going back to early high school, but nothing worth noting. It would have seemed quite odd if any of us wound up with another.

It was finally Sunday dinner and this time it was all just a mish mosh of leftovers. The day was casual. I think two of my cousins weren't there at all. I was pleased to see how mellow everyone was. It was soothing. As the night wore on, I knew it wouldn't be long until I told my mother. It was, after all, Sunday and those Sunday blues were about to kick in all on their own anyway. Heather and her family were the last to leave and my mom and I were still sitting at the kitchen table. My dad was in the family room doing his crossword puzzle, minding his own business, as usual. I was getting up to help clean the dirty dessert plates and clear off the table when my mother placed her hand on my arm. "Don't worry about that, I'll do it later."

"You want to talk now, huh?"

"I'm sorry. I can't have you leave this house not knowing if you're going to be okay."

"Well, Ma, I don't think I am. There, you know now, can I go?" I knew I was not going to stop there; nor was she going to let me. I was only half-joking when I said it though.

"Just sit." She guided me down to the chair with her hand still on my arm and her other hand on my shoulder. She knew I was ready to talk. I knew too. I started off slowly, going into every excruciating detail. I told her about how I allowed Todd to take over my client book and how I turned myself into his secretary. She was not necessarily surprised, as I had sort of alluded to it on several occasions. I admitted to the numerous drunken rampages and how sometimes I never had the courage to just leave. I had a hard time talking about the physical abuse, but I got through it all. I told her how there were times that I would go out and actually have fun and nobody would bother me. I told her what Todd and Josh specifically did to me. I told her every disgusting detail about the night of the holiday party and the lump on my head. I started and then couldn't stop. She never interrupted me once. Midway through this outpouring, my father had come in to the kitchen to get a glass of water and never left. And even then, I didn't stop talking about things that I would normally never speak of in my father's presence. About forty-five minutes later, I concluded my saga. My parents were both dumbfounded. They were speechless. It took a while for all of it to sink in. My father just put his head down and nodded in disbelief. The only thing that my mother could say was, "And when was all this?"

"Basically... all year." I continued to explain that I was drunk a lot of the times that these incidents took place, not to mention, they were after hours. If I even thought to make an official complaint to somebody, that would come back to bite me in the ass. Besides, who was I going to tell anyway? Could I trust Clark? Should I go to some random person in Human Resources? This was all too much information to be telling just any Joe Schmo at the firm. I questioned whether or not what happened to me was even wrong, or if it was my entire fault for ever allowing it to happen. Did I ask for it? I was very open and honest with my parents and told them exactly how drunk I'd get and how late I'd stay out with them. I couldn't candy coat anything. This was the real deal. Since I decided to tell someone, I was telling everything, no matter who it was. "Now what... what do I do? I can't work with these people anymore. I can't go back there but I can't tell anyone."

Even though I told them everything, I was still humiliated. It was a pretty creepy feeling telling my dad that my boss who was ten years my senior with a wife and children grabbed my ass and all I did was let out a measly chuckle. I didn't know if they were going to scream at me. I was afraid of being this huge disappointment. They were pretty understanding people, but I knew they'd never dealt with anything like this before. I was a puddle. I couldn't talk. I couldn't move. My whole body ached like I had the flu or something. It was as if I were feeling the strain of tensing all the muscles in my body for months.

"Call in sick tomorrow. Just for at least one day until we can figure this out." My mother had no idea what else to say to me at the time. Throughout the night I answered all of their questions. I still had sincere doubts about my innocence in all of this and repeatedly brought that to their attention. They insisted that I did nothing wrong and definitely did not deserve to be treated that way. I thought that since I was their little girl, they couldn't be completely objective, so I called Heather. I told her to come over. I wanted her opinion on everything. After she heard everything she was pretty shaken up. I couldn't believe this affected her so much. She said that she completely understood my concerns but assured me that there was still no excuse for that kind of behavior. I felt better hearing that from her as well. I also felt better knowing that I was not going to have to go there the next day. They all took this seriously, because they knew how seriously disturbed I was by all of this. They didn't doubt me for a second and made sure I knew that whatever happened they'd all be on my side.

None of us slept a wink that night. Heather ended up finally leaving my parents' house at around six that morning. That day, my dad stayed home from work and the three of us discussed what my next step should be. Heather came over later with the boys. She managed to squeeze in a nap earlier that day alongside Eddie when he went down for his. After hours and hours of rehashing, I decided that the best person to talk to was Clark. I felt like I could trust him enough and in the company bylaws, it stated that complaints such as these should go to your manager first. My father knew how he would handle this situation at his firm and how once a manager knows of such behavior, he is legally obligated to take action. He convinced me that the law does not allow this type of behavior and that Clark had to do what was right. Clark might not have even realized the extent of what was going on and could possibly appreciate my telling him. Nobody would want liabilities like Todd and Josh on his staff.

Chapter 8

I waited out the week through the new year and called to schedule an appointment with Clark. It was the first Monday following the holidays. I informed his secretary that I'd need at least an hour with him, possibly an hour and a half. She told me that an hour and a half was next to impossible if I wanted to meet with him any time before the President's Day long weekend. I surrendered to forty-five minutes of his time two Mondays from then. I was relieved to have gotten that over with. I felt like there was no turning back now. I had to go on with filing my official complaint. It was the best I had felt since I broke down and told my parents and Heather. My mood had been very solemn. I even passed up an all-you-can-eat-and-drink New Year's Eve party with my high school friends to stay home with my family. So unlike me. I had to answer a few questions from Marissa and Kristin. They didn't buy for one minute that I was sick. I told them that I'd be fine and that I was just tired from work. I lied and said that the end of the year at my office was crazy and that I had been working fourteen- and fifteen-hour days. The exact opposite was true. Trading volume was always low during those times. They didn't know any better and I took advantage of that. I also took advantage of Jill. The fact that she had a boyfriend made it easier for me to blow her off. I saw her on Christmas Eve when she and her family came over for dessert, but I never planned a specific night for us to hang out. Even when she mentioned to me that she'd most likely be moving in with Charlie officially, I shrugged and said, "We'll find the time soon." I refused to set a date with her. I simply didn't feel like it, and I didn't think she'd care since she had Charlie to occupy her time. It wasn't like me to treat my friends this way. I valued them so much and always respected them and here I was lying to them and avoiding them. I was changing and not for the better.

The next two weeks awaiting my meeting with Clark proved to be sheer hell. I was unusually quiet at work and avoided almost everyone in my life outside of work. My mother would call regularly, and I'd assure her that I was fine, but I'd consistently cut the conversations short. I'd do the same to Heather. At one point during those two weeks, Jill came back to the apartment to announce that she was moving in with Charlie. "Oh, wow. That's great news." I was lying on the couch wrapped in my Amazing TV Suit staring at the TV.

"You think? I'm nervous but excited. I don't know. I just can't believe it!"

"Yes, absolutely. I'm excited for you." I said monotonously.

"Are you really though?"

"Yes I am." My voice was trailing off.

"Listen, I don't want to pretend that I know exactly what is going on with you, but I think I have an idea. I know it has something to do with work and when you're ready to talk to me about it you will so... no pressure."

"Yeah, thanks."

"Elizabeth..." she leaned in to put her arm around me.

"Listen Jill, I'm sorry if I don't seem that excited for you right now. I'm just all out of sorts." I was truly happy for her, but I couldn't show it as much as I wanted because of how shitty my life was going.

"Huh, not quite the reaction I expected from my best friend."

"I know. But seriously, I am dancing on the inside, I swear." I don't think she believed me. And why should she?

She sat silent for a brief moment contemplating what she was about to say as if she was making a strategic chess move. "A best friend would be dancing on the outside, too, or at least would open up to me to explain why she couldn't." I sighed and rolled my eyes and didn't respond. She was right. And, on top of all the crap I was dealing with in my life, I was jealous of her. Things were falling into place for her. She had a life plan and was sticking to it. I, on the other hand, allowed my life plan to slip through my fingers. Things weren't going for me the way I had intended. Jill left the apartment in tears. By the time she left, I was crying too. I hadn't realized just how uninterested I was in my best friend's life. All I cared about was my solitude. I needed to wallow in my anxiety and misery. Jill was going to be back to the apartment one day that week. She mentioned that she'd take a day off from work to move. She and Charlie managed to get it all out in one day too. She actually had more stuff than I realized. The place looked surprisingly bare.

During those two weeks I was able to avoid going out to "entertain clients" only once. The other nights, I put my game face on and jumped in as if I weren't about to expose those jerks. I was careful to avoid complete intoxication. It was a lot trickier than I thought since most of these guys were often out to get me really drunk. It was a game for them. It was like their mission. I guess they thought I'd eventually do something stupid like agree to hook up with one or all of them or something like that. It never happened and that pissed them all off. To avoid getting too annihilated, I'd use a trick I learned in college. I had done this more often than I'd care to admit. After a few beers and a couple of shots, I'd excuse myself and venture off to the ladies' room. Once there, I'd induce vomiting before most of the alcohol could be absorbed into my system. It burned like hell but worked like a charm. I always had gum handy, so I'd pop a piece in my mouth, and head back to the bar. I had to do what I could to survive out there. I mean, I could drink a lot for someone my size, but some of those guys outweighed me by about two hundred pounds. Please do not try that at home, ever. It was extremely destructive and ridiculously stupid. But I had to stay as sober as possible. I had to have control of myself around these idiots.

That Sunday night before my meeting with Clark was a typical Sunday night for me, complete with panic attack and no sleep. I hadn't gone home for the family dinner and had passed up my parents' invitation to come in to the city and spend the day with me. My mom was uneasy about me being alone, but I assured her that it was for the best. My dad got on the phone with me to review everything he and I discussed about how to handle myself and what to say. He gave me a few words of encouragement and ended with a "You're doing the right thing." That's funny, it didn't feel quite right. When 5 a.m. rolled around I jumped in the shower and got ready. I lied to Todd and said that I had a doctor's appointment that morning and would be late. I figured that since Clark's office was nowhere near where we were on the trading floor, he'd never know. I was going straight to our meeting for nine o'clock. I left my apartment and went over to a coffee shop around the corner from my apartment and sat there reviewing my notes for two and a half hours before I headed downtown. I wanted to make sure I didn't forget any details. Not only had I documented the incidents, not only did I save the message that Josh had left on my voicemail, but I tape recorded the message as back up. I was lucky to have thought about copying it because it was the only physical proof I had of any of their shenanigans. Actually, I can't take the credit for thinking of recording it. My mother was the one who made me record it. I had played the message for her and my dad when I finally told them what was going on.

I'll never forget that morning. It was unseasonably warm for January. I had on a grey ribbed wool turtleneck sweater with black pants. I was hot as hell and being a nervous wreck didn't help. I had my hair slicked back in a tight ponytail and had applied a minimal amount of makeup to my face. I was too tired to bother. Once I got to the building, I was careful not to run into anyone from my group. It was pretty easy since most times we were glued to our phones anyway. I got up to Clark's office and when his secretary asked me what this meeting was in regard to, I told her that it was personal. She seemed concerned but didn't pry. I waited in one of the two chairs across from her desk outside his office.

When Clark opened his office door I felt my heart skip a beat. I swallowed several times to try to rid my throat of the huge lump that seemed to have set up permanent residence there that morning. When I sat down, he closed the door and plopped himself in the chair behind his desk across from me. I don't think he had any idea what he was in for. I started by telling him how much I appreciated him taking the time to see me and how important it was for me to talk with him. I was obviously scared and the slight concern on his face grew into outright apprehension when I asked him for complete confidentiality with what I was about to tell him. He agreed. I took out my three pages front and back of loose leaf paper but couldn't focus. My eyes were so tired they were burning. I blinked a few times, rubbed the insides along either side of the bridge of my nose, cleared my throat and began.

The forty-five minutes turned into two hours. Clark seemed sympathetic and concerned. He asked if I thought Rich knew what had been going on and I mentioned that he'd have to know something. I didn't think that Clark had any idea. He seemed befuddled and shocked. I believed him. I started giving general examples of the loose "locker room" talk among all of the guys. I felt like I was getting my concerns through to him. It felt good. He was embarrassed and ashamed. He apologized to me and assured me that he would have to take care of this. He thanked me for being so courageous. I was elated. He was going to help me. He called one of our employment attorneys and set up a meeting at his office for seven o'clock that evening. He asked me to leave the audio tapes and since my mother had made like eight copies of them, I agreed.

Bob Lynch, the employment attorney, was very diligent. He arrived at the meeting that night with pages and pages of information to review with me. He had the copy of the tape and notes from Clark. I asked him where Clark was and why he wasn't at the meeting, and Bob told me that he himself had to take over everything going forward. Bob went over the options for how to handle the situation. He asked me what I wanted to see happen to both Josh and Todd since they were the worst of the offenders. I told him that I didn't know what I wanted to happen to them and that I thought it was his job to determine proper punishment. I just knew that I wanted them to never do anything to make another woman feel the way they made me feel. EVER. I insisted on how significant discretion was because if word got out that I complained, my reputation would be scarred. Bob said that he would do everything in his power to keep them from talking. He mentioned that if they didn't comply with his rules, he could hit them with penalties that could go on their permanent records with the Securities and Exchange Commission. That was exactly what I wanted to hear. They could get fired and still not be able to tell anyone that I was the complainant because no matter where they would go to get another job, it would be on their records with the SEC. They wouldn't want that. They'd have to keep quiet no matter what. Additionally, when anyone who worked on the Trading Floor got either laid off or fired, the announcement was done away from the Trading Floor, usually in an office or conference room upstairs. Before they left for good, they were escorted back onto the Trading Floor by a security guard. They were not allowed to talk to anyone, look at anyone, or touch anything on their desks besides their personal belongings. They were instructed to gather up their stuff and then they were escorted out of the building. I asked Bob if I could be transferred to a different department in case word got out. I told him that I'd be willing to take a job at a lower level as long as I'd keep my salary the same. I figured it was the least he could do for me. There were thousands of employees in our complex alone; surely, I could be placed somewhere. He agreed that was definitely a feasible option.

Our meeting concluded around ten and I decided to take a cab home. I was too tired to trek over to the subway. I got back to my place and immediately called my mom. She and my father had been waiting to hear from me all day. They were relieved to hear how calm I sounded. I was excited that Bob had been so helpful, and they were thrilled to hear it as well. I went over all of the details Bob told me about their having to keep quiet with regard to everything that happened at the risk of ruining their careers. I mentioned how I agreed to take a job in a different department if necessary. My parents were a little surprised at that and argued that I shouldn't have to be the one to leave. I insisted that it was the smartest thing for me to do. I hadn't had a significant encounter with Rich outside of morning meetings since the debacle of bonus day, but I knew that if he found out about this, he would never treat me the same. I also knew that if Todd's little followers knew what I had done, they'd make my life a living hell. Even though Bob said that it was illegal for anyone to retaliate against me for what I had done, I still wanted to cover my tracks... just in case. I felt really good that night. I truly believed that the worst was behind me. I thought that down the line I might hit a glitch, but it couldn't have been anything I wouldn't be able to handle. I had never been more wrong.

Chapter 9

That next morning, I awoke after a very restful five hours of sleep. It was the most sleep I had gotten in a while. I was ready to face the day. I was prepared for the worst if Todd and Josh got fired. I had to admit, I'd have been happy with a scar on their permanent records or even demotions. Whichever, I just knew that their sleazy paws would never touch any inch of my body ever again. Their demeaning words would never cross these ears ever again. Maybe they'd learn how to treat other human beings with respect. Maybe they'd grow up. Maybe they'd be taught a lesson.

So absolutely nothing happened the next day and I hadn't heard from Bob at all. As soon as I walked through the door the following morning, though, I knew something was terribly wrong. Heading through the turnstiles right behind me was Andrea. I don't even know where to begin when describing Andrea. She was certainly a rare breed. She particularly had something against me, so others might not have seen her in the same light I did. When I first expressed my concern about Andrea to Roberta, Roberta had mentioned to me that she was tremendously insecure and most likely jealous of me. Such a "mom" response. She was pretty much the only other relatively young female in our department aside from a couple of female traders, and I was her competition. Well, I didn't consider her my competition, but she did me. I wanted Andrea to show me the ropes. I wanted to develop a trusting work relationship with her. She was another woman affiliated with our group and I longed for some female camaraderie, especially after Roberta was gone. She was only three or so years older than I was, but she had been around this group since immediately after college. Her family friend was the head of one of the trading desks. That's how she got the job. I think someone might've even created a position for her. Her family friend was that powerful. Actually, she wasn't even officially on our payroll. She was considered back office staff. She didn't have any trading licenses, nor did she have any desire to get one. She pretended like her job was the most important one and acted as if she was higher up in the ranks than she really was. I think everyone else caught on to her charade, but nobody realized just how evil she was. She was a discreet bully; like one of those calculating mean girls in high school. It was more just to me, one on one, with no witnesses. I wasn't the type to bad mouth colleagues to other colleagues. I knew better. I usually kept my opinions about Andrea to myself after Roberta left.

Andrea would talk down to me constantly. She would name drop in front of everyone like it was her job. She regularly spoke of her fabulous car, her designer clothes, and her perfect beach house in the Hamptons. She was so obnoxious about how spectacular she was. She wanted to remind others all the time that we weren't anywhere near as fantastic as she was. Andrea carried on about her prestigious family and how they all had memberships to the New York Athletic Club. Rumor had it that her dad was some big shot on the Stock Exchange. I think that's why nobody in our group cared about how bitchy she was. They were all in awe of who her father was and who her family friend was. It was like she had a "bitch pass." Andrea never confirmed or denied the rumor about her father, but she allowed it to swell. I, however, knew the ugly truth. It turned out that Andrea grew up in the same town where my sister and her family lived, and Andrea's family still resided there. Last spring, Heather stopped at the garden center in town to pick up some flowers and trimmings for the yard. She knew about Andrea and that her family lived in the same town because I had mentioned her to Heather on several occasions. Much to Heather's surprise, she learned that Andrea's family's company was the fertilizer supplier to that and many other garden centers in the tri-state area. Andrea had an extraordinarily distinct last name and it was plastered all over the garden center. They were, in fact, very successful. It seemed, though, that Andrea was completely embarrassed that her family business was shoveling horse manure. She owed her family money and prestige and stuck-up lifestyle to shit. Literally, shit. That just killed me. I never told anyone at work.

I wasn't completely sure why Andrea let her insecurities get the best of her. I guess we all lose control of them sometimes. She was no genius by any stretch of the imagination, nor was she a beauty queen. She probably never took any Series exams because she knew that she might not pass them. But she did carve out a nice little gig for herself (with the help of her family friend) and made herself seem irreplaceable. She carried herself very well too. She worked with what she had and made the best of it. She usually looked really nice and sounded like she knew what she was talking about.

Anyway, I'd see her the same time in the same place every morning and every morning, she would look away and pretend like she didn't see me. Or sometimes she would make that bragging small talk I mentioned earlier. That morning, she was almost delighted to see me. She walked over to me with this ear-to-ear forced grin on her face that reminded of Jack Nicholson when he played the Joker in the first *Batman* movie. I cringed when I caught a glimpse of her. It was actually kind of scary. She looked possessed or something. She greeted me with a pleasant voice and insisted that I go "grab a coffee" with her. It was all mostly small talk but before we went our separate ways once the elevator doors opened she gently placed her hand on my forearm and said, "Have a good day, hon." Hon? Was she feeling okay? That was so strange, why was she so nice to me?

When I reached the trading floor, I noticed that there were more people in at this time than usual and one of them was Todd.

Then it hit me. People knew. That's why Andrea was so nice to me and that's why Todd was here so early. I panicked. My heart started pounding and I couldn't catch my breath. I had to try to calm myself down as I slowly approached my desk. I thought that maybe I was just imagining that things were out of the ordinary. I thought that maybe I was just being paranoid. I wasn't. They knew. I couldn't understand how anyone knew, I only talked to Bob less than forty-eight hours before and I hadn't heard back from him as of yet. Clark, as the head of our division, couldn't tell anyone. It was stated in the company by-laws that if someone chooses to make an official complaint to the manager, then the manager can either take action or pass the information along to an employment attorney and completely remove him- or herself from the situation. Not to mention, Bob swore to me that he wouldn't take any action without talking to me first, so how could all these people know?

As it turned out, Josh got fired the night before. But they did nothing to prevent him from telling the entire desk that I was the one who complained. What happened to his security escort or not being allowed to talk to anyone as he's collecting his belongings and leaving? Evidently, Josh was upstairs in Rich's office, Rich fired him, and sent Josh right back down, unescorted, to collect his belongings. And it was then that Josh blurted out in anger to everyone who was still there for the day, that I was the one who got him fired. So much for protecting me. Oh, and what happened to Todd? Absolutely nothing.

That day turned into my worst nightmare. Nobody spoke directly to me but there was a lot of whispering and glaring. Some of the geeks of the group who obviously weren't in the know seemed fine towards me at first, but by noon, word had spread and even they didn't know how to treat me. The jerks and Todd followers threw nasty comments towards me under their breath in passing, and the nicer folks avoided me altogether so as not to associate themselves with the betrayal that was me. My two friends that I mentioned earlier, Tim and John, didn't care what anyone else was saying about me. They didn't let it affect how they were going to treat me. They were the only ones who were nice to me and made me feel a sense of safety. Unfortunately, they were not enough to make things easier for me. I couldn't focus on anything all day except fighting my tears. I wanted to disappear. I wanted to go back in time and erase the last two days. I made a huge mistake. I should have never filed the complaint. I wanted to just up and leave. I wanted to go home to my parents. I wanted to retreat into a tiny ball on the couch in our family room and cry my eyes out until I couldn't cry anymore. I didn't. I stuck it out. I thought that I had to remain strong.

I had placed two calls to Bob that day and he never returned either one. Clark, of course, was at some off-site conference for the next three days and according to his secretary was unreachable. That was most likely a big load of crap. I didn't know what else to do or who else to turn to. Almost everyone at work was against me in some form or another. At five o'clock on the nose, I picked up and left immediately. I don't even know if I finished what I needed to or not. I just had to leave. As I was approaching the elevator and the doors were opening, I stepped in but turned immediately because I heard someone behind me. It was one of Todd's minions. Under his breath, he muttered something unintelligible and spit on me right before the elevator doors closed. I instantly began bawling uncontrollably... the ugly cry, complete with snot flooding my philtrum and all.

When the doors closed, I was in the elevator alone. The type of people I worked with really sank in at that moment and not only because someone just spat on me. I couldn't help but stare at the elevator buttons. I had noticed this before but it really resonated with me at that specific moment. My mind was immensely focused on this, even after what had just happened to me. The "Close Door" button was completely worn down, while the "Open Door" button still looked shiny and immaculate. I felt like this truly represented what so many people in this building were like, always in a hurry to get where they had to go themselves and would never take a brief moment to help out a fellow human being by holding the door open for another person. In those few moments on the ride down to the lobby, I imagined how many times someone was running for the elevator door and whomever was inside was frantically pressing the, "Close Door" button so as not to waste a few seconds of their precious time. It was as if their time were the most important and nobody else's mattered. I was the type of person to hold a door open for someone and those buttons made it clear that I was in the minority. It seemed so intensely and strangely significant to me at the time.

I raced off the elevator and into the lobby. I flew passed Sorel, one of our security guards and my friend, without so much as a wave. I felt awful because he was one of the nicest human beings I'd ever encountered. I'd never whip by him without a wave, smile, hello, or quick conversation. I'd always bring him coffee because he couldn't leave his post. Some days during down times, I'd chat with him and learn all about his wife and three children. He worked two jobs. He was also a doorman at an Upper East Side apartment building at nights. I knew I'd have to answer to Sorel when I saw him again. When I made it out of the turnstile into our building's main promenade, there were several groups of tourists scattered about. I darted through the middle of one of them and headed to the public restroom. I went directly over to the sink and wiped the collar of my coat where the spit had been sitting and began absorbing into the wool. Then I splashed some cold water on my face before heading back out in public.

I rode the subway back to my apartment while there was an endless flow of phrases running through my head. I had never been called a "fucking cunt" or "manipulative bitch" before that day. And I was just hearing it over and over again. I couldn't believe how people were so quick to turn against me without even knowing all of the details. I was surprised to learn that more people didn't take my side. Everyone knew deep down that Todd was scum. Everyone knew what went on in that group day to day. Everyone knew, but nobody would advocate for me. I thought that if I spoke up and people did find out that it wouldn't be that bad because the disgraceful behavior of some of those men was common knowledge among our group members. It was amazing. Almost everyone had treated me like I was the villain for some reason. They all knew that Todd had it coming and that he should have been stopped a long time ago. They were all under his spell now more than ever. Even most of the "geeks" saw it as an opportunity to get "in" with him. They figured if they struck me down in front of him, he'd take notice and open the doors to the inner Todd sanctum so they could hop right in. Who could blame them? It was the only way to make money in this group. But they'd never get in. I mean, I was living proof that you couldn't let just anyone in on the secrets that surrounded Todd and his disciples. If anything, Todd was going to be more careful now about whom he let in.

Bob finally got back to me that next week after seven more follow up calls and said that he had no idea how Josh was able to leave the way he did. He said that once word got out there was nothing that he could do and that I should just keep my mouth shut, my head down, and my nose to the grindstone. That was actually a lot easier than I thought, since almost nobody was speaking to me anyway. I begged him to move me out of that group or put me on a leave of absence or do something to get me out of there because it was like torture. He told me to proceed "business as usual." It had been over a week since our meeting and he said that a few details needed to be worked out and that he would notify me as soon as he finalized the details of my case. I told him that it was not fair to leave me there and allow me to be treated the way I was being treated. I asked him about the illegality behind retaliation and why he hadn't done anything to the people who are retaliating against me. He said that I was overreacting and since I was in a sensitive state, I might have been imagining or embellishing some things.

"Don't patronize me, Bob. What the hell is going on here? I've had to sit through this torment for almost two weeks now. Why are you telling me you can't do anything for me? I thought you were on my side here."

"Elizabeth, calm down. I am on your side. The law forces me to be very careful with my decisions. I have to proceed with caution here so as not to disturb business."

"Huh, really?" I said, completely dumbfounded. "So you're on the company's side and not mine then?"

"That's not what I meant!" he snapped back.

"Oh, really? What did you mean, Bob? Because it sounds to me like you don't care one bit about what I am going through day in and day out here. You can't even begin to imagine what it has been like for me these past few days. I have been a freak show to my colleagues, Bob. They sit there and whisper and stare at me. They've disconnected my phone line so I can't answer calls. My computer conveniently crashes every hour on the hour so I can't get anything done. Our morning meetings have been held a half an hour earlier and I was never notified of the time change. They are making it impossible for me to carry out my duties. Not to mention, they are blatantly antagonizing and ostracizing me. What are you going to do about all of this?"

"Elizabeth, listen. I am doing my best here. We are completely understaffed and I have a lot on my plate right now."

"That's bullshit Bob. I want real change here and I want it now!" I was fuming. I could barely control my anger. I had never felt like that before. I imagined it being like a volcano just before it fully erupts. I actually think I had steam coming out of my ears.

"Okay Elizabeth, I promise I will have everything wrapped up for you by the end of the week. I will take care of Todd and the retaliation for Josh's firing. I realize that you are extremely upset, and you have every right to be."

"Alright, thanks Bob."

Chapter 10

Two weeks had gone by since my initial complaint and wouldn't you know it? Nothing else had been done. I headed into the weekend without another word from Bob or anyone. Clark came back from his off-site conference for about six seconds when he had to fly to DC for some big cheese convention, so he was no help to me. In fact, I don't think I'd ever seen or spoken another word to him ever again.

Monday morning approached quickly but my Sunday blues had been slightly alleviated when Heather volunteered to sleep at my apartment. She drove back ridiculously early Monday morning before the kids woke up. I knew how much of a pain that was for her and appreciated it tremendously.

When I arrived at work, I fully expected to have to leave a strongly worded message on Bob's voicemail when Rich came down an announced an emergency meeting at nine o'clock. It had to be about my situation, but I hadn't heard from anyone about what was going to happen.

Everyone filed into the conference room in complete silence. Bob was there and so was this Human Resources manager, Dean Stevens, who had been helping Bob with my case. My heart was pounding, and I could feel my face getting flush. The beads of sweat were beginning to form at my hairline and my hands were trembling. The meeting had to be about me and Todd and Josh; what else could it have been about? I didn't understand though, Bob said that he would notify me when something else was going to be done. Would they actually proceed without filling me in? As a matter of fact, they would. Rich began.

"It turns out that a very courageous person came forward with some information regarding our client outings. We all know and appreciate how difficult it was for her to do this. It was the right thing to do." Holy crap. I would have liked some warning if he was going to get that specific.

"We need to reevaluate how we are spending our work time outside of the office and how we are spending the firm's money while doing so. There will be no more client dinners without my consent. There will need to be at least one member of our team present for every client. We need to minimize any chance that situations could get out of control. Please know that entertaining our clients is part of our job and it cannot be completely eradicated. I do promise to make these entertainment ventures more conducive to everyone on our team." Okay, now what? Was he going to field questions here?

"We need to close the book on anything regarding past client outings. We need to stop all of the gossip and scuttlebutt that has been surrounding any recent incidents and return to business as usual. This is all over and done with and we need to make a fresh new start. We are moving on from this. It was a minor speed bump in our group's road to having a successful business year. Thank you, this meeting is over." What a freaking worm. Was he serious? Was that all he was going to say and do? No more action was taking place? I didn't get it. That couldn't be it. It wasn't just about the client outings. Not only that, but now I was the asshole who took away all of those wild and crazy client outings. Just then Rich motioned to me to come over to him. Bob and Dean and I all sat down near Rich and then he began explaining to me what was going on. Josh was fired and all the action that they needed to take was taken.

"And what does that mean exactly?" I asked.

Rich proceeded, "Well, it's a big deal that Josh was fired. You got someone fired, isn't that enough? What more are you looking for here?" I GOT him fired? He didn't do this to himself? I couldn't believe what I was hearing.

"Well, was anything filed with the SEC on Josh's record?" I was hopeful they at least got that right.

"Well, no, that's really not up to us, now is it? He is no longer employed here and what he does from here on out, we have no control over."

"But I thought Bob said..." I tried to finish.

"Bob was misinformed."

"So, Josh can just go out and get another job at another firm at any point from here on out without any future employer knowing what he did?" And I wanted to add that Rich and Todd would probably give him glowing recommendations, but I refrained. I was in shock.

"Is that all?" Rich was getting immensely impatient now.

"I... I don't know. I don't know." I was so confused. I was hoping there was more. I was hoping that something would happen to Todd. Did they just eliminate the weaker link and think that'd cover what Josh and Todd had EACH done to me? "But, what about Todd?"

"What about Todd?" Rich countered.

"What's going to happen to him?" I was honestly confused.

"Well, Elizabeth, you see, in cases like these, it's your word against his. We really cannot take any action with Todd. You had proof about Josh, we really had to do something about him, but you had no proof at all that Todd did anything wrong. He's been a big part of my team at BSJ and our previous firm. He'd been enormously successful. It'd be extraordinarily difficult to get anyone to believe that he was anything but professional towards you." It seemed as if they decided to have Rich do all of the talking because he was using his spectacular intimidation tactics on me. I was scared to question him. Since he was such a puny man physically, he had to make up for it with this gigantic terrorization. It worked. It was like when I met with him for my bonus and raise numbers. He said what my bonus was and that was that. He had a roundabout answer for every one of my questions then and the same was true again now.

95

"But what about a warning for Todd? What about a probation?" I probed, noticing Rich's discontent.

"There is no need to put this incident on his permanent record. We have to be careful. He may turn around and sue the firm if we take any sort of action that is too harsh. You see Elizabeth, this is the way a big firm like this works. You can never be too careful. Now, you did the right thing and it was very brave of you to stand up and speak out. You should be proud of yourself."

"Um, okay... thank you?" I sputtered in sheer confusion. I thanked HIM... again! "But what about all of this retaliation? What about the fact that everyone has made my life a living hell for the past two weeks? Isn't it illegal?"

"Elizabeth, you are a smart young woman, I think you knew those risks coming into this." Rich gave me a fake sympathetic look. "Besides, after that speech of mine, nobody is going to bother you. There is no need to rehash and backtrack; we need to move forward from this." His glare went through me like daggers. He was so pissed that I ever brought this up. I ruined his perfect kingdom of money making and I had been paying for it for the last two weeks. There was no reason that he couldn't have come to this conclusion in five minutes and end my horror sooner. He wanted me to suffer. He wanted me to pay for what I had done. He wanted everyone to see what would happen to them if they snitched just like I did. He wanted to use me as an example to others to deter them from complaining. He was very successful in doing so. If people didn't really hate me for what I did, they now were scared to even be seen near me, so I was completely isolated. He was purely evil and loving every minute of it. He knew he had the employment attorney and HR manger in the palm of his hand because he and his group were money makers. Bob and Dean didn't have power over him. They were problem solvers. They cost the firm money. In the end, the business side of the company always had the power.

"Thank you for your time, gentlemen." Rich shook Bob's and Dean's hands, collected his belongings, and darted out of the conference room.

"Are you kidding me with this?" I was astonished that they sat back and watched that entire chain of events take place and did nothing.

"Elizabeth, listen, our hands are tied here. There is nothing we can do anymore," Bob said in a low somber voice. With that, I stormed out of the room. But not before I assured Bob that he would be hearing from me again.

Standing outside the door I'd just slammed, I felt good. My heart was pounding, but I felt strong. I had stood up for myself against Bob and Dean. But that made me wonder why I was still so meek with the real villains. I think it was because, when I spoke to Bob and Dean, I knew it could actually have an impact. With the others, I knew that standing up to them would get me nowhere or worse. I was more comfortable with Bob and Dean and could express myself honestly to them, because I could tell each had a conscience.

After a few more weeks of less blatant torture, I called Bob to request a meeting with him and Dean. I had been documenting all of the incidents in which I felt I was being exposed to a hostile work environment. It was so hard to describe to people who weren't there what it was like for me to continue working in that group. I once again began doubting myself. I doubted that what had been happening to me was even wrong. I doubted myself as a competent employee and doubted my good nature. Maybe I did deserve the shit I got from everyone before and after my complaint. Maybe I asked for it; every bit of it.

I didn't even have to excuse myself from my desk, or tell anyone where I was going, because nobody even acknowledged my existence. Immediately after Rich's meeting that day, we had a new seating chart. I was placed in a row away from the rest of our group. I was sitting with some of the international traders who had nothing to do with what I did. It was deliberately inconvenient. Nonetheless, it made it very easy for me to disappear on so many levels.

Bob and Dean agreed to meet me in the other building of our complex so as not to risk being seen by anyone in my group. I appreciated that. This meeting was surprisingly fast. All I had to do is mention that I spoke with my parents and they recommended that I speak to outside counsel who specialized in employment law. I was bluffing. Bob shot a quick glance over at Dean and then looked back at me with an indescribable stare. "Really Elizabeth? You think you are going to hire an attorney?"

"Yes, I think I may." Still lying. "There were so many things you guys should have done for me but didn't. You really screwed up, and now I am paying the consequences, and that is not fair."

"Well then, it sounds like your mind is made up. Why did you need to see us again then?" Bob asked still with that bizarre look in his eyes.

"No, Bob, my mind is not made up. I don't want to have to do this. I want us to work this out. I'd hate to take such drastic measures. Please understand that I know deep down you guys really want to help me, but the politics of business are getting in the way. I want to give you another chance here. You can help me. I know you're on my side, please."

"Sorry Elizabeth," Dean murmured. "I think you know what you need to do." I was floored. Was I reading them correctly? Did I follow what they were trying to do? Were they almost telling me themselves to hire a lawyer? Were they allowed to do that? When they both saw that I realized what they were doing, Bob brought his hands up to his chin, closed his eyes and gave me a silent nod. I gathered up all of my documentation and began heading for the door. Dean stopped me, "Elizabeth..."

"Yes?"

"I am authorizing a medical leave of absence for you. You look awful. You need to get out of here for your own health and safety."

Bob chimed in, "I know this should've been done weeks ago, but we will discuss opportunities elsewhere in the firm for you. Call me next week and we'll set up a meeting. In the meantime, go home and get some rest."

"I want all of this in writing before I leave this room." I was adamant. I was not about to get any more screwed than I already had been. I got what I needed, went back to my desk, picked up my bags and left for the day without even turning off my computer.

Part Three

Every Dog Has His Day

Chapter 11

During my leave, I went and stayed out at my parents' house. We did some research on employment attorneys. Being that my father was in the industry, we had an array of prospects from which to choose. We couldn't figure out if a larger firm with greater resources and a stronger name would be best or if the more personalized attention of a smaller place would benefit my case more. After all, we were up against a Wall Street powerhouse.

Initially, I consulted with two larger firms which proved to be a complete waste of time. The first attorney repeatedly named a different large Wall Street corporation as my employer. After I corrected him for the third time, I kindly thanked him and immediately excused myself, leaving a three hundred fifty dollar consultation fee behind. After that disappointment, I had to muster up enough energy to try again. Since the previous attorney had seemed so uninterested in my story, I gathered that my case was not that strong. I began to speculate if I even had a case at all. I was petrified of putting myself through further humiliation.

The second of the two larger places I went to was even worse. I set an appointment with one of the partners. His credentials were impeccable, and he seemed very attentive over the phone when I arranged for the consultation. In person, however, he seemed way too attentive to the unnecessary details of their inappropriate behavior and found some of it humorous. He was too interested in what was specifically done and how things were done to me physically rather than focusing on the fact that I actually was discriminated against, retaliated against, and harassed by my boss and colleagues. For instance, when he would ask about the circumstances surrounding Todd smacking me on my ass, he had a slight grin on his face and asked if it hurt. The way he was inquiring made me feel extraordinarily uncomfortable. It had such a creepy vibe.

"I don't mean to sound rude, but in the grand scheme of things, some of these details do not seem critical enough for us to be discussing at this point."

"Well, if I am going to agree to take this case, I have to know as much as I can about your situation." He could tell I was getting frustrated. "It sounds to me that taking legal action here would just be a waste of your time and money anyway. You also wouldn't make a strong witness since you were out cavorting and getting drunk with them."

"I beg your pardon? I don't think you are really listening here. There is much more to it than that." I was shocked.

"Well, in the state of New York there is a three hundred thousand dollar cap on the amount of damages you can collect in a sexual harassment lawsuit. And we won't be able to take any critical action until after the Equal Employment Opportunity Commission gets the chance to review your case and that can take up to six months. So, what we are looking at here is a whole lot of waiting for not a whole lot of monetary reward."

"My concern isn't just about the money, it's about making sure they don't do this to anyone else again. I am beyond them abusing just me. They need to learn how to deal with a complainant better. They need to understand that the way they treated me after I spoke up was wrong, too. There is more to this than just the sexual harassment and abuse." I had to admit that I was disappointed that the most they'd be required to pay me was a mere three hundred thousand dollars. That would be like when I drop a penny under the counter at the 7-11 and don't bother picking it up. That's crap. That's pocket change for them. I wanted it to be enough money to affect them with the hopes of changing the culture of some of the groups within the firm. I knew that every department wasn't like ours. I knew there were really respectable men who worked there. I knew there were trading desks that treated women equally. Wait, I don't want to get ahead of myself, treated women respectfully.

"Listen, Miss Graham, you're naïve to think that it isn't about the money. You are also naïve to think that you can change them. It's always about the money with the huge corporations and there is nothing you can do about it." Could he really be right? After all, he was the attorney, he would know. But still, that wasn't fair. I wanted to get my chance to stand up to them. I didn't want to give up. I wanted to fight for every woman who has walked through the doors of BSJ & Co. who didn't get the same chance as her male counterparts. I also wanted to prevent future mistreatment of female employees. But who was I? I was only one person. How much could I really change? Well, I knew I wasn't going to be able to do it with this man's help. He was a pervert anyway.

Even though I knew he was the wrong attorney for me, I felt awful. I was horrified. I completely regretted ever saying anything to Clark in the first place. My situation was hopeless. I was a fool to think that any good would have come out of filing an official complaint. I hated hearing my parents and Heather telling me over and over again that I did the right thing. It sure as hell didn't feel right. It couldn't have felt more wrong. I just destroyed my career and it was too late to turn back. What was I going to do? I couldn't return to that job. There was too much irreversible damage. I was seriously considering resigning. I thought I would just escape from BSJ & Co. for good and put it all behind me. The more I reflected on the various horrible incidents, the more I realized how stupid I had been. I let these men treat me this way. I allowed myself to get drunk around them. I sometimes even had fun with them and danced with them. I was as much at fault as they were for everything. I was stupid to think that all this wouldn't turn back around on me.

I had frequent flashbacks of the worst nights. Certain smells and sounds triggered physical reactions. I couldn't ever wear the perfume I wore the night of the holiday party again. I sprayed it on myself one night since, and I actually gagged. I couldn't stand the smell. I tried wiping it off with a damp cloth, but the scent still lingered. I ended up having to shower all over again. I also couldn't ever hear Josh's favorite song, because he would always play it on the juke box at Sami's. It never failed. Every single time we went there he had to play it. It was his favorite. I couldn't even listen to the first three notes without instantly breaking out into a full-on sweat or getting the shakes. I cringed at these thoughts. Sometimes I would get so upset recalling those events that I would cry. Other times I would get so angry that I'd want to punch a wall. Either way, I was miserable and ready to give up. I felt like it was hurting me. It was hurting me all over. I was emotionally drained and losing sleep. My body was actually aching with grief. I wasn't sure if I could continue the battle. I was trying to cope with the trauma that I was experiencing but was barely hanging on by a thread. But then I'd swing in the opposite direction and think I was being overdramatic and weak. I realized I needed help, professional help.

I had actually gone to a therapist at my family's urging. One of my sister's friends had recommended her and we'd met only three times at that point. It had potential. She was perfectly fine and I'm sure a great therapist to others, but I didn't feel like our sessions were particularly helpful to me. It was in between all of these attorney appointments when I realized that finding a therapist, like finding an attorney, was like dating. Some worked, and some didn't. I had to "date" other therapists to see if they worked.

That was when I met Dr. Alice. Marissa recommended her. A fellow nursing student who was also a friend of Marissa's and lived in the city sang Dr. Alice's praises. I thought I'd give her a try, and if she didn't work, I'd just keep researching and "dating" until I found a better match.

I quickly learned that I didn't need to look any further. I

recall being absolutely petrified right before my first appointment with Dr. Alice. She shared office space with another doctor, but when I got to the waiting room it was eerily desolate. I arrived early so I had to sit there in my agony and wait. It would have been fine had the waiting room actually been more conducive for such a thing. It was tiny and completely dull; not the least bit calming. The entire room was approximately ten feet by twelve feet. It was rather stuffy. There were no windows and thus no circulation. The walls were painted a drab white and there was grey wall-to-wall indoor/outdoor carpeting. There were three folding chairs and two small tables. One of the tables was in the center of the room that was supposed to create the coffee table effect but was nowhere near the size of a real coffee table. The other taller one was immediately to the right of the door when you walked in. The table by the door had a small lamp on it that didn't really project much light, even in such a small room. After about fifteen minutes of staring at the walls, I heard some rustling sounds and voices coming from her office door. When I couldn't hear them clearly is when I noticed the noise machines on the floor in either corner of the room. My sister had them in the boys' rooms for when they slept. These noise machines were designed to prevent people outside the therapy room from overhearing what was being discussed inside. They emitted the strangest sound. It actually sounded like a louder version of the noise you hear when you put a seashell up to your ear, which we all know never really sounded like the ocean. Her office door opened suddenly, and two women emerged. As they said their goodbyes, my nerves really started to kick into high gear.

Dr. Alice was an amazing woman. She was very gentle and sweet. She was soft-spoken to the point of seeming shy, but she was not shy by any means. When she and I first met, she was so welcoming that I felt I had already known her. I wasn't ready to get into too much detail right away and she urged me to talk only when I was ready. That was very comforting to me. I hated talking about everything that went on. Talking about it made me feel like it was happening all over again. I spoke of my experiences in small doses to Dr. Alice and that helped me cope with the agony of repeating it. "I couldn't help but feel that I had this coming," I finally admitted.

"Elizabeth, blaming yourself for something that you can't go back in time and change is not going to help you." She was right. But I needed sympathy. "What you went through was completely shitty and it doesn't sound like it's anywhere near over."

"Yeah it was shitty, but I could've done so many other things to avoid being a victim."

"You are a victim," she assured me. "You put your trust in these people, which you should have done, and they took advantage of you on so many levels. There is no excuse for how anyone in that office behaved."

"I hadn't really thought of it that way." I didn't realize that there was a complete breach of trust. It was true. I trusted Todd, Rich, Clark, Bob, Dean, and BSJ & Co. on the whole, and they all let me down.

"You were not supposed to go into that job expecting your boss to take advantage of you. You couldn't have predicted that you would have to defend yourself against these people."

"I could have defended myself better," I retorted.

"You shouldn't have to defend yourself like that at your job. You were treated unfairly. Don't be ashamed to admit that."

"I feel like such a whiny brat."

"I understand why you would, but you should try your best to get over those feelings. I'll help you with that. You should not have been put through what you were put through and even the strongest woman out there would have faltered somewhere along the line. They ganged up against you; nobody would have won that battle. Something bad happened to you. Accept it and I'll help you learn to deal with it." I heard what Dr. Alice was telling me, but I hadn't really felt it yet. Logically, I could understand her, but my emotions had trouble believing her. I didn't want to be one of those girls who didn't get what she wanted so she would sue her company. Actually, that I believed that girls routinely sued their companies for not getting what they wanted just proved how much help I needed. So I had a hard time with the idea of a lawsuit, but I also knew that there was no way that I could go back there. I knew I'd have to quit my job. The leave of absence was just buying me time.

I was starting to feel worse and worse every day. I missed my friends, especially Jill. Jill and I hadn't spoken in over a month. She had absolutely no idea what was going on with me. Marissa and Kristin would check in with me and I'd lie and tell them that I was doing fine. They'd pass on my love to the guys and I'd swear that I'd hang out with them soon. I'd hear all about their recent adventures and wish that I had enough energy to go. They all took a ski trip to Vermont for a long weekend. Normally, I'd be all over that, but I just hadn't been feeling well enough. Being that Brian and Susan were engaged, it was the six of them hanging out together. It used to be the six of us. That was hard for me to swallow and I was bringing it on myself.

Chapter 12

I had been almost ready to give up, but my mother convinced me it wouldn't hurt to try one more attorney. Here's a cliché that's actually true: third time's a charm. When I arrived at Julie Birch's office, said third attorney, I was greeted with a warm, comforting smile. I got a great vibe from Julie, just like when I met Dr. Alice. I started to call her Ms. Birch and she promptly threw me a, "Please, call me Julie." She knew of my situation only what we were able to squeeze into a five-minute phone conversation, but I immediately felt like she was on my side. She started off by explaining to me that she understood how difficult it was for me to even see her. She knew that it would be hard for me to tell my story again. It was like she knew what I had been through. She had this calming presence about her. She wanted me to feel at home and wanted me to be at ease. I could tell that this was going to be a completely different experience than the other two I'd had. Birch and Steinman was a smaller law firm, and I got a great feeling from that. Julie had a very nurturing way with me. In the past, I had felt ashamed about telling my story. I was scared that I had nothing to fight. I wasn't scared with her.

She was very petite and quite attractive. She stood a mere five feet tall and had great skin and a beautiful smile. She had to be around fifty because there was a wedding picture on her desk where the bride had to be her daughter. She looked like an exact replica of Julie but twenty or so years younger. It could've been Julie herself if the quality of the photo didn't look so current. She had a great sense of style. Her voice was very stern and projected very loudly, which I could only imagine was of tremendous benefit in the courtroom. She saw that I had all of my notes dated and organized and was ready to talk. Just before I got started, she asked if I wanted coffee and asked her assistant if she would please get us some. We made small talk until the assistant returned and Julie's office door was closed. I was hoping that this would be the last time I would ever have to tell my story ever again. I was reliving it every single time I told it. I didn't know how many more times I would be able to talk about it. None. This was it. If Julie didn't want me as a client, I was giving up. I couldn't take it anymore.

I began. I first discussed with her how once Rich and Todd took over as our new management team, I noticed the changes in my daily responsibilities. I mentioned how Todd had pulled all of my accounts right out from under my nose. I told her how at bonus time, I overheard Josh and two of Todd's other followers talking and laughing about how everyone else got screwed out of bonuses except themselves. They were almost admitting that they didn't deserve more money than the rest of us but were happy to take it. I reiterated that the overall vibe of the group changed and not in a good way. I gave her a feel for the fraternity environment, so she could really grasp what I was explaining. All of this led up to our discussion of specific incidents during our client outings.

Since I had noted and dated everything in chronological order, that's how I read it all back to her. She sat in complete silence without any interruption. "At first, these client outings seemed harmless. We'd go to dinner, have a few drinks and laughs and call it a night. I was actually excited about them. I loved going. I felt important. A lot of our clients really listened to me. I shared my ideas and they liked what I had to say. I got through to them. I had solid investment plans and they bounced their ideas off me and we collaborated. It was fascinating for me to feel so important. As the weeks went by, everyone noticed that these clients would call our desk and ask to speak with me. I think this bothered some people. Todd and Josh and a few of the others in the macho club realized that I actually was a threat. I was good.

I was smart, and I worked well with people. I think I was refreshing for our clients. I dealt with them in an honest fashion which was not the way the others on my desk did. This was when Todd took it upon himself to step in.

"Instead of simply not inviting me to client dinners, they figured they'd invite me only so that they could humiliate me in front of everyone. One of the first specific times I could recall this humiliation was when we had gone to one of the best steak houses in the city to wine and dine one of our top clients, Bud Hempstead, who flew in from Texas for one night with us. Afterward we headed to this swanky piano bar. I couldn't remember exactly what I was discussing with Bud, but I'll never forget when Todd came over to us.

'Hey, why don't you go on over and get Bud another Dewar's.' Todd was looking right at me.

'Um, excuse me?' I was puzzled. 'The wait staff here is really very good.'

'Well, I see that his glass is almost empty and if it's not a bother, we would really appreciate it if you could just run over and get him one now.'

'But we were just...' I couldn't even complete my thought. Bud sat there in silence.

'Thanks, Elizabeth. We really appreciate it.' I hadn't really thought much of it at that moment. Then I got up from the table, and Todd quickly reached around and slapped me on the ass. 'Atta girl.' Todd said with a patronizing smirk. 'She's so good to have around.'

'And mighty fine to look at too.' Bud chimed in.

'Yeah, she's a keeper.' Todd spoke about me as if I wasn't even in the room.

"I noticed how Bud's impression of me instantly went from impressive, smart, young woman to nice piece of ass and Todd's gopher. It was amazing how Bud took cues from Todd. If Todd didn't think highly of me then there was no way that our clients would. Todd knew that. Todd intentionally treated me like that in front of our clients so that they wouldn't take anything I had to say seriously. It began happening on a regular basis after that. As soon as Todd would notice that I was having a one-on-one conversation with any of our clients, he would instantly step in and humiliate me in some form or another. It actually got to a point where he would have one of his other lackeys 'covering' me throughout the night, so I was certain not to get any one-on-one time with any of our clients. I was still determined though. I didn't let them get to me or give in right away.

"After a while the nights out became very routine. I would struggle to prove myself to everyone and sure enough, someone from my group was always there to undermine what I was saying. The guys I worked with had it down to a science. They all knew what they had to do to me and they had fun doing it. It was a game for them. One time I even overheard Josh say that he was not on 'Elizabeth duty' tonight. That drove me to fight even harder to prove myself. It got tiresome very quickly though. Soon enough, I made every attempt not to attend any of these dinners, but they all failed. I would lie about having a doctor's appointment or volunteer programs after work, but Todd would tell me to cancel them. He said that I had no choice and that if I expected to advance my career, I would have to go the extra mile. If he said that he wanted me there, I didn't have a choice. It was weird because I knew it was all bullshit, but I would listen to him anyway." I couldn't explain it any better to Julie, but she nodded to me as if she understood.

I continued. "Another regular occurrence was how Todd and Josh had this bizarre competitiveness for my attention. It was as if they had a bet going to see which one of them could get into my pants first. The whole idea was sickening to me since Todd was married and Josh was, well Josh. I was always amazed when

I would see Josh successfully 'pick up' a woman, which he did a lot. His lack of hygiene alone made it practically impossible to have a conversation with him, no less hook up with or sleep with him. He must've lied about the money he was making. While it was far better than what I was making, it wasn't what I imagined the women who hung out at these Wall Street places expected. Anyway, Todd and Josh were often very competitive when it came to me. I would notice one of them watching if the other was talking to me or feeding me shots. I was their prey and neither one of them was going to let the other have me. It was very uncomfortable and when I couldn't manage to slip out and go home, I'd have to lie about being nauseous and threaten to vomit on their shoes if they didn't let me leave."

One night I was able to escape, or so I thought, and Josh actually got in a cab behind me and followed me back to my apartment. I hadn't noticed when I first got out of the cab, but as I got to my doorstep, I heard him barking at the cab driver. I turned around and he stumbled up the curb toward me. He was disgusting. He was so drunk he could barely stand up. He begged me to talk to him while professing his love to me, again! I told him that he needed to find a cab that would take him home, but he told me that none of them would drive all the way to Long Island where he lived. Just as I was going to hail a cab to take him back to the bar where I was certain Todd and a few of the others still were, he grabbed my arm and tried to kiss me. I panicked and screamed, 'What the hell are you doing?' I told him that we have been through this before and he needed to stop doing this to me. I was furious. He told me that he knew I wanted it and that I should just give in. I was so aggravated and clearly struggling but he kept on pulling me toward him. I yelled at him to stop and told him that he was causing a scene, but he didn't let go. When I cursed at him, the loudest

"Fuck you" I could muster up, he released me. We both stood there in silence for a brief second and when I realized that I was free from his grasp, I ran back up to the door of my apartment building. He followed me, and I fumbled with my keys but managed to make it inside and slam the door in his face. For the next hour and a half, he kept calling me and ringing my buzzer. I ignored it, hoping that he would go away, but he persisted. I turned off my cell phone and finally told him over the intercom that I was going to call the police if he didn't leave me alone.

'Fine, go ahead.' He yelled back at me. So I did. I made it out to be a mere noise complaint when I called. The buzzing didn't stop for about another twenty minutes and when it did I clicked the listen button on my doorbell to try to hear what was going on. It was all garbled and muddled so I couldn't decipher what they were saying. I heard the words, 'sir' and 'officer' but that was about it. Whatever happened down there worked because he didn't bother me the rest of the night. I was not about to go down there to find out anyway.

"The next few weeks Josh was a complete jerk to me. He would find any reason to yell at me in front of everyone. Some people, including Todd, noticed that he was only acting that way towards me, but of course nobody ever said anything to him about it. He was Josh. He could get away with it. He also got away with yelling at me in front of some of our clients. One night he caused a scene and started bitching me out for something ridiculous. I couldn't deal with everyone in the bar staring at us, so I stormed outside. When I confronted him and asked him what all of this was really about, he denied any ulterior motives for yelling at me. I told him that he was full of shit and that's when he let it all out. He gave me that whole speech about, 'Who the hell do you think you are for passing up a guy like me?' He accused me of thinking I was too good for him. I told him that I simply didn't think there was chemistry between us and that I also didn't date people that I worked with. He acted like I should be grateful and jump at the chance to date him. It was so degrading."

I also mentioned to Julie that Josh seemed to have been stalking me. "Two mornings, on my way to work, he appeared at the end of my block just standing outside the corner deli. When I asked him what he was doing there, since he lived in Long Island, he mentioned that he had a friend who lived in the area and that he had crashed at this buddy's place the night before. One Saturday afternoon, I was going to get a manicure and there he was again! He said he was with that same friend but for some reason this friend never had a name or a face. It was rather creepy if you ask me."

I was about to get into the worst night of them all, the night of the holiday party, when I had to pause and take a deep breath. This incident was the final straw. I had a huge lump in my throat, so I swallowed a few times and began.

"As the party was winding down, the group of regulars was rallying together. I was wondering why we had to even go anywhere else at all. The party was enough, wasn't it? That night, it was the normal group including one of the other female traders, Ali. Once in a while, she'd come along on these nights out. But she rarely ever acknowledged me, so to me, it was like she wasn't even there. Todd certainly didn't seem to pressure her about it being part of her job, though. She was a bit older and more established at the firm. And she definitely didn't seem like as much of a pushover as I was, maybe that's why. As we were all climbing into the limo, she mentioned to me that we were headed to a pretty exclusive lounge.

"Like, how exclusive?" I asked.

"Like celebrity exclusive," she responded with a smile.
"Really? Can we actually get in to a place like that?"
"Of course we can! Why would you even think that we couldn't?" She spoke to me like I was a moron. In retrospect, I suppose that was closer to the truth than not. Here's another cliché, Hindsight is twenty-twenty. I have to admit, at the time, I was actually a little excited to see what this posh club was all about. Besides, Ali was there with me. Even though she wasn't ever super friendly towards me, I was still glad she was there. Maybe the guys would bother her for a while and leave me alone. I was hopeful anyway.

When we pulled up to the place, it looked exclusive for sure. It was all black out front, with no windows and a red velvet rope leading up to the door. I gathered that if celebrities frequented this establishment, it'd have to be as discreet as possible. I'm sure none of them would want paparazzi getting shots of them stumbling out after a night of drinking. We all hopped out of the limousine and the bouncer opened the door for us as we filed in. Immediately through the door was a maitre d greeting us. 'Hello, Todd, good to see you again. Hello gentlemen, and ladies, welcome. Can I take your coats?' Oh so fancy this place was! I felt so important. Maybe this night wouldn't be so bad after all.

There was a long hallway to our right with black curtains and gold and silver sparkles on it. As we walked down, I could hear the music getting louder and louder. Then we rounded the corner and as I gave the enormous open room a quick glance, I immediately realized where we were. It was a gentlemen's club; complete with body glitter and thongs and tassels. 'Oh my God, Elizabeth, oh my God, play it cool.' That's all I continued to tell myself. When I looked over at the others, they were all chuckling, including Ali. I just kept telling myself not to look or act surprised. I suspected, though, that my uneasiness was written all over my face and they loved it.

We gathered around a few small mirrored tables in these chairs that looked exactly like ones my parents had in their 1970s living room. I wanted so desperately to pretend like I was okay with all of this. I wasn't. But for a while, I played along, probably not hiding my disdain very well. I don't know why I cared so much what they thought of me. I cared that if I didn't go along with it, I wasn't cool or something. Seriously, JUST like in high school. How could I be such an imbecile?

Despite the fact that there were naked ladies with trays ready and willing to serve us drinks, Todd handed me his card to go up to the bar. "The usual," he said. I was fine with going up there because I took the opportunity to do two or three shots without anyone noticing, in order to calm my nerves a bit. It wasn't like me, but I was super uncomfortable and thought it was a good idea at the time. They hit me pretty hard and fast. I made small talk with the bartender for a while to avoid going back over to my group. I was usually very good at recognizing when I had to stop drinking, so I did. It might've been a little too late though. I never do that, I never let myself get too drunk around these guys. What was I thinking? When I finally returned to my seat with Todd's drink, there was a mostly naked woman waiting next to it. As I sat down, I gathered she had been waiting for me. She leaned in and asked me if it was okay for her to dance for me. My heart sank, and I had this enormous pit in my stomach.

Giggling out of sheer panic, 'Oh, you know, you are so beautiful, really, and thank you for asking, but I'm good. Really, it's okay, thank you, but no.' The rest of the group roared with laughter. I rose from my chair instantly, 'Alright, I'm super drunk and I need to go home!' I was. I just had to leave. Enough was enough. I was the dork who couldn't hang out with the cool kids and I was absolutely okay with that at this point. The room was spinning anyway. I was really drunk. I was half embarrassed and half enraged. The rage was at myself. What was I even doing there? Ali stood up as soon as I did.

"It's okay, are you alright? It was just a joke, it's all good now." I shockingly sensed the slightest bit of remorse in her voice. A joke? Really? I remember when I had a boss whose idea of humor was putting my stapler at an eighty-five degree angle instead of ninety. That was a joke.

"No, I am actually really wasted, and this music is really getting to me and I really need to go. I'm headed out, good night everyone, have fun. I'm good, I'll just catch a cab." I picked up my purse and darted back down the long hallway to retrieve my coat. By the time I got outside the door into the crisp air, I immediately felt better, until I realized that Todd was right behind me.

"You okay?" He asked seemingly genuinely.

"I'm fine. I'll just get into a cab and go. I'm tired anyway. I really don't need to be here." I never let myself get too drunk around these guys. What was I thinking? After a few shots and a bunch of martinis at the party, I knew that even the full stomach I was drinking on wasn't going to help me sober up.

"Come back inside. Come on, it's fine, it's just fun."

"Um, no, really I need to go. I'm a lot drunker than I thought and I need to go."

"Not yet, don't leave." He tried to persuade me. I had a very foreboding feeling at this point. With that, he came a lot closer to me and pulled me towards him. His wandering hand made its way to my ass as he tried to kiss me.

"Oh my God, what are you doing? Stop!" I was half mumbling, since his lips were pressed against mine. It was so blatant. I was astonished. I looked up at him in sheer horror and he was smiling. I cringed at that same smile that I once thought was so charming.

"What, come on, let's go. I'll leave with you." He sounded oddly calm.

"Umm, no." At this point I was really anxious to get the hell out of there and get home.

"Come on, nobody's out here, nobody will even know." Then he tried to kiss me again.

"Stop it, I'm going home ALONE!" Why ever did he think I wanted to do this? What in God's name did he think was going to happen? Now I was in a full-on struggle with him but he had a pretty tight hold on me. It sounded like he thought it was funny. I heard some chuckling amidst my struggle. Then I raised my voice, 'STOP IT!' In response, he took me by the back of the head and grabbed my hair and wrapped it around his hand like he was pulling on reigns. He yanked my head back so hard I saw stars.

"Come on!" He said grinning through his clenched teeth. It was like he was whispering and shouting at the same time.

I was dumbfounded. I had no idea how to respond to this. He'd been a manipulative jerk before but never this physically aggressive. I was really scared now. I should've screamed but I couldn't.

He looked at me with some bizarre combination of anger and amusement and said, 'Let's go.' I sat there stunned like a deer in headlights. It was then that I realized that he didn't care about what I wanted or didn't want to happen. 'Let's go.' he repeated almost nonchalantly. When I looked up at him, I still had no idea what I was going to do. I felt even sicker and before I could say anything the vomit flew out of my mouth and all over him. He immediately pushed me off him, shouting profanities, including but not limited to, 'What the fuck?' and 'Fucking prick tease!' I fell backwards onto the ground and smashed my head against it. Part of me was so relieved on so many levels.

But most of me was still petrified. It was as if I had spewed my poisonous venom at him in defense. My head was throbbing at this point, too. I hit it hard. I must have turned my head during the fall because the side of my head was in the most pain. I know he didn't mean for that to happen and he looked at me in utter shock to see if I was injured.

"I'm fine." I mumbled. I thought maybe he felt a tinge of guilt and would be apologetic.

"Yeah, you're fine, you're okay, get up." He didn't even help me. He wiped some of my puke off of himself with his bare hands and shook the residue off onto the sidewalk. Then he reached into his pocket for his wallet. He threw forty bucks at me while I was still trying to get up from the ground. The bouncer came over by where we were.

"Are you alright, Miss?"

Todd answered for me, "She's fine, totally fine, she just had too much to drink tonight. I'm getting her in a cab now. Don't worry." He was laughing and basically shooed the bouncer away.

"I'm fine, thank you." We were a little farther from the door where the bouncer stood. There was a small alcove where his post was, so I guess he hadn't really seen or heard all that much. He reluctantly walked back, looking at me as if he was waiting for some sort of signal for help.

My head was pounding, and my knees felt weak. What in the hell was happening? I could barely see straight. I was a mess, I was scared, and in the moment all I could do was contemplate how I could have handled all of this better. What was going to happen at work on Monday? Todd walked out into the middle of the street and whistled for a cab. Within seconds, one pulled up, and I watched from my hands and knees on the ground as he started making his way down the street. "You'll be fine," he mumbled as he walked away. I managed to stand but was hunched over, making my way to the street because my legs were practically incapable of holding me up at that point.

"Here, let me help you." It was the bouncer.

"Thank you, really, you are so very kind. I appreciate it, thank you." I climbed into the cab, closed the door behind me and thanked the cab driver before even telling him my address. When we pulled away from the front of the club, I watched as we passed Todd, with his ridiculous saunter and his eyes forward. It almost made me throw up again."

Julie was astonished. She couldn't believe that my manager and the attorney did nothing about this.

"I take only one in ten of the cases I hear, and I will take yours." I sighed with relief. I felt a warm feeling come over me as I immediately burst into tears. I thanked her profusely.

"Are you sure? Are you sure I have a case? Was I wronged? Can I actually do something about this?"

"You were absolutely wronged, and you can absolutely do something about it." She quashed any doubt I had about all of this being my fault. She made me feel better about wanting to fight. She was very forthcoming about this not being an easy battle. She said that I would find it hard and may want to give up at times. She needed to know if I was fully prepared to handle what was ahead. I assured her that I was ready. I wanted them to pay for what they had done to me.

We briefly discussed what was going to happen next, and she laid out the timeline of how things were going to unfold. She mentioned that all correspondence between me and anyone at the company would go through her. I told her that wouldn't be a problem since nobody there talked to me anymore anyway. She told me that I would have to endure a lot of waiting. The legal process would take time and I had to know that none of this was going to be resolved quickly. She mentioned that we would do everything in our power to avoid going to court because then we'd be looking at years and years of dragging this out and I'd have to relive everything several times over.

Chapter 13

I had been off on medical leave for a couple of weeks when Dean called, through Julie of course, to tell me that there was an opening in a different division but at a comparable level with my previous job. That whole day proved to be a complete waste of time. I met with this horrid woman who acted as if she was the only successful woman on Wall Street. She made me feel like I was wasting her time. As soon as I mentioned that I had been working for Rich Miller, it was as if a light bulb went off in her head. I was "that girl." She had heard. She knew. It was a huge corporation but a small little world. She puckered back up and fumbled around for words to cover her sudden realization, but it was too late. She saw my discontent and then played it off. "Well, we don't think you'd be a good fit in this group. It seems that your lack of experience in how our division is run is a complete hindrance."

"I see," I told her. I knew that if I ended up going on any more interviews, they'd all turn out this way. Stories like mine travel fast. I couldn't wait to leave her office and head back home. On my way out, I was wondering how it was ever going to be possible for me to work at that firm again. I didn't want to transfer to any other branch office; this was our headquarters. This was where it all happened. It was the center of the action. This was where I wanted to be. I shouldn't have to leave. Why should I? Before I exited our complex, I quickly stopped to see my favorite security guard and friend, Sorel. When he asked where I had been, I told him I wouldn't be returning but didn't explain why. He respected my privacy. I hugged him and cried and escaped before anyone in my old group saw me.

I called Julie and told her what happened. She immediately contacted both Bob and Dean. She urged them to cooperate fully and work together on finding a resolution or there would be a lot more trouble from us. I was glad she was so stern with them. I shouldn't have to have gone through all of this, and if they did their jobs right in the first place, none of this would have happened. Bob and Dean were strapped. There was really no way for them to undo the damage that had already been done. Even though they promised that they'd find a place for me elsewhere in the firm, they couldn't promise that wherever I went, people wouldn't already know what had happened.

I began to realize that it was practically impossible for things to ever pan out smoothly if I were to stay at BSJ. I had to make a decision regarding whether or not I wanted to go back. Julie advised me that it had to be my decision and my decision alone. Neither she nor anyone at the firm should have any influence on it. For the benefit of my wellbeing, I concluded that I should not go back to work anywhere at BSJ & Co., and once this mess was over, I'd officially resign.

When it came time to decide how to approach our fight against a huge corporation, I was rather confused. I didn't want to sue them for money, nor did I want to report any physical abuse to the police. At the time, this was all difficult enough. I didn't want to have to deal with a criminal case too. The incidents were way too after the fact, and I didn't want any information about them to be public information. I just wanted both Todd and Josh punished with more than a slap on the wrist. Julie emphasized that big Goliath corporations only understand money. There was no way to force them to fire Todd, but if I requested damages, they'd pay up. Julie told me that I had to come up with a number that would satisfy me. I had to put a price on the sheer hell that I had put up with. I had to come up with an amount of money that would make me feel vindicated. Where to start? Hmmm, let me see. What's the going rate for humiliation these days? What's the price someone should pay for making you feel like a useless waste of space? I had no idea how to figure any of this out. I asked Julie for some figures on cases similar to mine. The problem with that was when people settled out of court, the amounts were never disclosed.

"You have to figure a number that's good enough for you, so I can figure out a higher number to start the negotiations." Julie seemed like she'd be stern and solid and a good woman to have on my side.

"What about this NY state cap of three hundred thousand dollars on sexual harassment and discrimination cases that the other attorney told me about?"

She explained, "There are different types of damages and only one type is capped."

"So I may be able to ask for more than an amount under that cap?" Woo hoo!

"Well, within reason, Elizabeth. You are still young and very capable of finding another job. That's what BSJ will say. They're not just going to throw cash at you to keep you quiet about what happened." Okay, Julie. Even though I was told I couldn't include lost future earnings because I was young enough to find a new job, I sure as hell considered it.

"But they should. Why would they want this to get out? If money is what it comes down to, then they should have to pay. I've already had to accept that Todd is not going to get fired or penalized more severely otherwise. I've had to accept that it's only about money. Why can't they accept that I deserve enough or I'll talk? I'll call the newspapers if I have to. I don't care!"

"They have the upper hand because they know you won't want to go to court. They are using your vulnerability against you. They know that you'll have to eventually settle because you'll want to put an end to all of this and you won't want to have to relive it. They know that you don't want your name and these incidents public. I know it doesn't seem fair, but this is what we are dealing with." I could feel Julie's sympathy as she was explaining all of this to me.

"I wish they could just fire him and this would be over." I wished a lot of things at that point. "I know we can't make them fire him, but how can we even make sure they don't treat anyone else like they did me?"

"I can't guarantee you anything, but I can promise that I will do everything I can to help you." Julie was trying so hard to comfort me.

"Why aren't we taking them to court again? Why did you advise against that?" I honestly had forgotten.

"Well, you've been through enough trauma already. Going to court would only make you feel more pain. I have to look out for your overall wellbeing. Besides, it is a typical tactic for big corporations like this to drag your name through the mud to destroy your credibility."

"Right, now I remember... I was drinking with them, out late with them, blah, blah, blah... I was a drunken slut and I deserved what I got."

"Well, I'm also concerned about them saying you were never even qualified for the position you held in the first place. Todd was smart when he took over your accounts, he basically turned you into his assistant and they would have no problem countering our claims of sexual discrimination. They would say you deserved to make less since your responsibilities were less important than the other men's."

"But I did hold the same position as those other men. Todd wormed his way into my account book and was my boss, so I couldn't really do anything about it. Isn't that illegal?" I was getting so frustrated.

"That will be extremely difficult if not impossible for us to prove, Elizabeth. I'm sorry. Todd was very manipulative and very careful about it."

I noticed just how severely this was all affecting me. I was not feeling well emotionally, psychologically, or physically. I couldn't handle the waiting. When Julie said that it was a lengthy process, she was not exaggerating. We had to file our complaint with the Equal Employment Opportunity Commission and give them six months to evaluate and investigate it. However, the EEOC was so backlogged with cases that there was no guarantee that they would even get to my case during that six-month period. Unfortunately, before we filed in court, we had to wait that time frame, no matter what. In the meantime, I'd have copies of affidavits sent to me to sign and notarize, phone calls from Julie or her assistant requesting specific details about some of the events that took place, and friends and family constantly asking me about what was going on. It was all so frustrating, but I settled in for a half-year process.

My parents and Heather were obviously very well kept in the loop as my case progressed. Since I wasn't working, I was staying at my parents' house for most of time in the beginning. I didn't want to be alone and as usual, their house was my comfort zone. My cousins and my aunt and uncle were slowly filled in on the details. My friends were beginning to get suspicious when I wasn't returning phone calls or emails or making any effort to hang out with them. I missed them terribly, but didn't have the energy to go out. Plus, I was not about to get into the gory details of my ridiculous work, or lack thereof, situation. Since Jill and I weren't really on speaking terms, it was kind of easy to avoid her. How terrible that I was actually relieved about that.

Eventually my friend Steve wasn't having my vague conversations. The more I made up excuses not to go out, the more he called me. Eventually I gave in to him and Kristin coming over to my apartment. From then on, I actually did hang out with them, and it was nice. Out of all my friends, they were the ones who actually knew most of the details. Steve, Kristin, and I would make our way to my apartment in the city some weekends and we'd go around the corner to a local bar in my neighborhood. It was late spring, almost summer, so the three of us would go to Kristin and Brian's parents' house down the Jersey shore for weekends when nobody else was using it. I'd spent all the summers of my high school years, and then all my summers after high school, going back and forth to that house. Most times, it was with a big group of friends, but this more recent, more intimate group was really nice, too, exactly what I needed at the time. These weekends at the shore coincided with the Triple Crown horse races. There was a racetrack down the shore that had live racing on Kentucky Derby, Preakness, and Belmont days in the spring, and then every weekend throughout the summer. Steve and Kristin taught me how to bet on the ponies. I was clueless. I ended up picking horses based on the numbers they wore. Probably not the best way to do it.

Either place, the city or the shore, we'd usually end up just drinking too much. But some of our funniest moments came out of those nights. One time, when the three of us were down the shore, we had been up really late just hanging out at the house. We were marathon drinking, talking, and laughing. It was the kind of laughing that doubled as an ab workout. Without explanation, Steve got up mid-conversation to turn the clock around so we couldn't see the time. Kristin and I completely understood why he did it. It then became a regular thing when we were chilling out at the shore house or at my apartment and having way too much fun together. I loved that so much.

I looked forward to those nights with them. I didn't have to get ready to go out anywhere fancy. I could just throw on a tee shirt and jeans and throw my hair back in a ponytail. It wasn't stressful being with or talking to them. It was important for me to spend time with them. The more intimate setting was much easier for me to handle. It was actually all I could handle at the time.

At first, I thought that I was managing all of my free time very well. I helped my mom around the house and with errands. I arranged to sit for my nephews twice a week, so Heather could actually get some work done. Before she had the boys, she was working at an advertising agency in the city. She was so valuable to them that they set up a nice part-time work from home gig for her while the boys were still little. I would also stop by on other days and watch the boys so she could get some everyday chores done or treat herself to a manicure or something like that. It was kind of nice for me. Since my mom didn't work, I always found something to do with her. I also managed to do some research on a local soup kitchen. They needed volunteers who were available for daytime hours.

The soup kitchen was run out of a church basement. It was only about twenty minutes away from my parents' house, so I was able to go usually twice a week. When I first started there, I was helping with their homeless breakfasts. I remember on my first day it was the end of May and it was about a hundred degrees outside and probably 98 percent humidity. The organizer and head of the parish, Father Ray, was concerned about our visitors getting dehydrated. He asked if I would hand out extra water. He had this cart and I had to wheel it around to all the tables and make sure people got what they needed to stay hydrated. I quickly became known as "water girl." All the volunteers and the homeless people referred to me that way. It was actually kind of funny. It was very superhero. I liked the sound of it. When I was working with the soup kitchen, it helped me to feel better. I felt useful and as if I was contributing something important to society. It helped me cope with what I was dealing with.

I couldn't stave off the depression, though, no matter how many shore nights and soup kitchen days I filled my time with. I turned to eating to help me cope. I wasn't sleeping well, maybe hour and a half spurts throughout the night, so I was literally eating around the clock. I'd wake up and go downstairs and just stand in front of the open refrigerator door. I'd stare and stare until I'd come up with some random concoction of whatever was in there. If I was out during the day, I'd often hit a fast food drive thru. I'd of course eat it in my car, so I could throw the evidence right in the receptacles in the parking lot. I'd pull away from the window and pull right over to a parking spot. I felt like a drug addict, only my drugs were burgers and fries. I just kept telling myself that since I was miserable, I deserved the pleasure I got from food. I didn't fully understand that I was self-medicating and was perhaps beginning to overdose.

Gradually, I started staying alone in my apartment more and more. I found it much easier to not have to lie and explain myself to anyone about how I was feeling. I was sick of faking being okay so as not to worry my parents. I wanted to wallow in my sorrows. I wanted my own space and didn't want to deal with anyone. This was a bizarre feeling for me. I sought isolation. I'd never sought isolation before in my life. I always chose to surround myself with people I loved. I used to think that the alone time I got in the shower every morning was enough alone time for me ever. I couldn't understand why I wanted to leave my safe place, the house I grew up in, but I did. For a short amount of time, being with my nephews and Heather and my mom, and Steve and Kristin, and volunteering at the soup kitchen, were things that I looked forward to and helped me. But I was so overcome by negative feelings; even those things weren't a priority for me anymore.

When Julie finally informed me that we set a date for a formal mediation to reach a settlement, I was relieved. I had been waiting for this all autumn and winter. I saw the light at the end of the tunnel. The mediation process was relatively simple. It was one side versus the other side on neutral ground with a neutral person to oversee us and help us come to an agreement. The neutral person is an employee of a mediation corporation. I couldn't believe that I'd survived the last year or so since I made my initial complaint. It felt like it had been ten years.

Chapter 14

Julie had prepared me for the worst. She told me that I'd have to tell my entire story over again to the mediator and that we might not finish this in one day.

"Wait, we're meeting at nine in the morning and we have until four that afternoon, and you're saying we might not finish this in one day?" I was utterly confused.

"Listen, Elizabeth, their proposed terms may be very far off from our terms, and it can take a lot of time for us to agree somewhere in the middle."

"Okay, I understand. Do they feed us?" Geez, what was wrong with me? I was dealing with one of the most difficult things in my life and all I could think about was food?

"Yes, lunch is provided," Julie chuckled. "Are you alright? Are you ready? Do you have any questions?"

"Yes," I lied. "Yes," lied again. "No." Yeah, what kind of menu is it?

I hadn't slept a wink the night before the mediation. My mom asked if I wanted to sleep at home and she'd come in to the city with me and hang out and clean my apartment for me while she waited. I told her I was fine. I didn't want her there. I wanted to stress out all on my own. When I left the apartment to head to the mediation, I stopped for a jumbo coffee to get me going. I was probably better off being so tired I couldn't think straight. That way, I really could only think about how to stay awake and not worry about what the day ahead held for me.

I met Julie outside the building, which was way downtown. It was a brisk morning in April. I couldn't believe that it took me over a year to get to this point in the battle. I was all bundled up to keep warm, but my palms and underarms were soaked with sweat. Julie greeted me with a warm smile and an even warmer hug. She asked if I was ready to head in or if I still needed a minute before continuing. "I'm ready, let's do this." I told her that I wore my most comfortable pants suit so if we had to sit there all day, I was prepared.

"Please begin, Miss Graham." The mediator, Ms. Simmons, seemed very smart and diligent. She lacked compassion, but I guess that's part of her job. She made me a little nervous at first, but once I started talking, I managed to get my story out without any major breakdowns. Bob and Dean were there representing BSJ. I couldn't even look at them. The good thing was, once both sides stated their cases, we were then separated. Bob and Dean stayed in the large conference room where the beginning of the session took place, and Julie and I were jammed into this teeny room with no windows, one small round table and three chairs. We started. Julie told Ms. Simmons our proposed terms and Ms. Simmons brought it over to Bob and Dean.

While we waited the first of many long waits that day, I took off my suit jacket, slid off my shoes and nestled with my legs up on the chair. My heart was pounding. How did this all happen? How did I get here? Why were we fighting about papering up settlement terms? The real reason to fight was lost in all of this. I couldn't believe I allowed myself to agree to mediate instead of resolving this before a jury in a court proceeding. What about all of the other women I wanted to fight for? What about doing everything in my power to change the way women were treated? What about paving the way for future young women so they have fewer road bumps to face? I felt like such a coward.

The first time Ms. Simmons came back into the room, I was beyond frustrated. I was ready to walk out right then and there. "Screw them. I'll see them in court." I was crying already. Julie had her arm around me, hugging me.

"Elizabeth, we have to stick with this and really try here. I'd like to remind you that the point of today is to come to an agreement and end this nightmare for you." Ms. Simmons was right. I did want this to end today. It was just so frustrating. For a brief moment I wondered what it would be like if we did take them to court. I could stick it out. I could fight. I could fight for me and for every other woman that ever walked through the doors of BSJ who was treated as terribly as I was. I could definitely handle it. I'd love a huge dramatic ending with a jury finding them guilty and laws being changed. I would want to make the rights of complaining witnesses stronger and better. It could be the case to change those laws. It could be history and I was in the position to help change them. Julie had mentioned at one point that I would make a good witness. Hmm, how much worse could it really get?

"Elizabeth, I know what you're thinking." Julie interrupted my fantasy. "Please trust me that you don't want to go to court. I absolutely cannot tell you what to do; I can only advise you on what I think is best. Please know, though, that at this point whatever you decide, I am right behind you no matter what. I would fight for you in court just as hard as I am fighting for you now. It is your decision, but I am looking out for your best interests. I've seen what this case has done to you so far and this isn't even half of what we'd have to go through for court. Do you want to proceed with today? Because if you do, I'd need you here wholeheartedly."

"I completely trust you, Julie." I did. "Let's go." The mediator went back and forth from our room to Bob and Dean's room several more times. There was more back and forth than I think either party expected. Ms. Simmons informed us that they had to make a phone call in order to get approval each time we counter offered after their initial offer. Julie told me that was a good sign. They were usually given a hard line coming into the day, and if they had to call someone during this process, it meant that they were going above what they initially were permitted to give me. I was happy to hear that. Every time Ms. Simmons returned and I heard that doorknob turn, my heart sank. What were they coming back with? Was it even close to what I wanted? It was so stuffy in that windowless room and that added to my suffocating feeling; that and my sweaty palms and underarms. To dry my hands, I kept rubbing them against my pants along the top of my thighs. I must not have realized just how hard I was pressing because my hands began to burn from the friction.

Six hours and a scrumptious deli sandwich later, we reached a settlement. I was pleased with the settlement terms. I honestly couldn't believe it was over. I breathed a huge sigh of relief and immediately began crying. It was one of the best cries I had had in a while. The settlement was enough for me to feel secure during this next phase of my life. I could take time off, figure out my career, and maybe even do something fun that I've always wanted to do. I wasn't quite sure what that would be just yet, but I knew it would be good, really good. I immediately called my parents. They were so relieved that I felt good. That's all that mattered to them.

Outside, I cried and hugged Julie for about twenty minutes. The second I released Julie from my intensely grateful grip, I glanced over her shoulder. I saw Bob and Dean exiting the building looking utterly defeated. Their shoulders were slumped over and their heads hung. They were completely disheveled. Their ties were loosened and their hair looked tousled. I caught Bob's eye. He gave me a little smirk, and turned away and headed down the street. I knew they weren't the real enemy in all of this. I actually felt sorry for them in that moment.

I didn't want to leave Julie for some odd reason. We decided to go celebrate and have a drink. It was nice being with her at a happy time. She and I were both so relaxed. We talked about so many other things besides the case. I asked her about her family, specifically her daughter in the wedding photo on her desk. It was nice to get to know about her outside of her work and I know she felt the same about me. "Julie, I can't even begin to tell you how much all of your hard work means to me. This was a huge life crisis and you helped me through it more than you could ever imagine. I am going to miss you being a part of my life. Wait, actually, no offense, but I'm glad you won't have to be anymore."

"Oh Elizabeth, not to worry. There is still a lot of finalizing that needs to get done, so you won't be getting rid of me that easily."

Chapter 15

During my first two sessions with Dr. Alice following the mediation, I was elated, and she loved to see me happy. I told her how great it felt to have won this fight that I thought was never going to end. I told her how excited I was to move on with my life. I thanked her profusely and reminded her that I couldn't have gotten through this without her. She reminded me that I still needed to focus on getting well. This was a huge step in that process, but there were still a lot of things that I needed to do to take care of myself. I assured her that I wasn't going to let this settlement interfere with the long-term progress that I needed to make.

"Elizabeth, please keep in mind that it took about a year and a half to break you down and it all can't be fixed in one meeting." Dr. Alice was being extremely cautious.

"I know, I know, but I do feel great. I can't explain it. I just know that I am okay. Everything is going to be okay." Ahhh, now there was a cliché I loved saying. Why wouldn't it be okay? The settlement had brought finality to the legal dispute. I was going to see a career counselor and was excited about finding a new job, one that was more fulfilling. I also had Brian and Susan's wedding coming up. It was a destination wedding on a small British Virgin Island, so my friends and I were all going down there for an entire week!

My family and friends were relieved to find that this was all behind me. I didn't get into too many specifics with too many people because it wasn't really anyone's business, but I managed to get enough detail in so people got the gist. I was eager to start hanging out with my friends again. I wanted to make up for all of the lost time. I thought, at least for a short time, that everything really was going to be okay.

The trip for Brian and Susan's wedding was an absolute blast and couldn't have come at a better time. It was honestly one of the best trips of my life despite it being bookended by the most traumatic situations of my life. The two of them headed down a little earlier with their parents, so Jim, Steve, Marissa, Kristin, and I all traveled together. Steve and I were the most organized of the bunch, so everyone put the two of us in charge of arranging the details. Steve handled the rental villa and I handled the flights. It ended up being more efficient for all of us to fly to Puerto Rico and charter a small plane from there.

Marissa had her Xanax for the traveling since she was a nervous flyer. The minute she saw our little propeller plane in Puerto Rico, I thought she was going to have to down the entire bottle to avoid a nervous breakdown. "Oh my God, could that plane BE any smaller?" Insert high pitched voice. The plane sat eight people including the pilot. We were all seated in height and weight order with the tallest and biggest being in the front of the plane and the smallest and lightest being in the back. Steve was the tallest, so he had to sit up front next to the pilot. The plane was so tiny that during take-off and landing, Steve had to move his knees out of the pilot's way so the pilot had access to all of his controls.

When we landed and Marissa kissed the ground, it was a short ride to our villa. And boy did it not disappoint! Great job, Steve. It was enormous and open and beautiful with a huge living area, dining area, and kitchen. The entire back wall of the house was one giant sliding glass door with views directly out to our veranda, pool, and the wide breathtaking ocean just beyond it. Off to the right of the living room were two bedrooms. The decor was your typical bright colored island decor and it was uplifting and magnificent! Once we stepped outside onto the veranda, it was like an entire second area of living space. There was a large section with an outdoor living room set and a huge grill to the right and another dining table that sat twelve people to the left. Just beyond the dining area, there was another building that was all part of our villa. It was two stories and on each floor was a huge bedroom with a walk-in closet, enormous bathroom and an outside shower. Marissa and I took the downstairs room of that house. When we settled in, I took a deep sigh and couldn't think of a better place to be at that time.

Throughout the week, more and more wedding guests were arriving on the island and all of our villas were in the same general area. There were a few family villas, two villas with each of Brian and Susan's respective college friends, and then our villa. Our villa became the party house, aka "The Jersey House." Each night there would be talk amongst the guests about how loud the Jersey house was and how they all wanted to check it out. I guess we were all just so excited to be there together and celebrating, we got carried away! We'd have our Bon Jovi and Bruce Springsteen blasting on the speaker that Steve brought with his iPod, some new music device he had that none of us had ever heard of. We were playing drinking games on the huge outdoor dining table. Throughout the week, random people, some wedding guests, some not, would come onto our veranda off the beach and we'd all just yell, "HEY, come on over!" The more the merrier. It was so much fun. And we did this for six straight nights.

The guys were usually up first in the mornings and making breakfast for us, which was awesome. Steve was getting so frustrated because none of the stores he went to ever had enough ice to keep cold the obnoxious amounts of liquor we had. There also seemed to be a shortage of matches or lighters on the island too that we needed for all the cigar and cigarette smoking that everyone seemed to do that week. In fact, Steve decided at one point during the trip that he was just going to stay and live on the island and open up a store called, "Fire and Ice" and all he would do is sell bags of ice and lighters, literally, that was it.

The wedding night itself was beautiful and the calmest one

of them all since it was the final night that we were all there. Leave it to Marissa to be the one to leave us with the most memorable moment of the week. She had been flirting with and hooking up with one of Brian's college friends during the trip. As we were all winding down in the outdoor living room area back at the Jersey House, they wandered off onto the beach. It was night time and they decided to go skinny dipping in the ocean. We all knew where they were and the guys, of course, were making jokes and being all immature. We all chuckled along though, it was harmless banter. Suddenly, we heard a loud scream. It was Marissa, immediately followed by her high-pitched squeal, "Something BIT ME!" I swear, we were all laughing so hard most of us had tears rolling down our cheeks. I immediately got up and ran over to the beach to see if she was okay. Trying to hide my laughter, I darted to where she was standing and as she was fumbling to throw her dress back over her head, she shouted, "Oh my God, Elizabeth, LOOK!" I honestly didn't expect to see much. I figured she was exaggerating, which she often tended to do. But oh my God was she right! It was a welt the size of a baseball that had instantaneously turned black and blue...on her right butt cheek! Of all places, whatever it was had to bite her on her butt cheek. As if she wasn't going to get enough grief about everything already. We went back to our room, where I gave her an ice pack and some medicine to take for the pain. She was half crying, half laughing at that point. "It figures," she said. "I have to sit on two different planes for over four hours tomorrow."

"Not to worry," I responded. "I'm sure the swelling will go down by tomorrow and you'll feel a lot better." It did, and we were laughing all the way home the next day even though we were sad that the amazing week ended.

The result of the mediation and the high from the trip proved to be a mere adrenaline rush. It wore off quickly and my depression hit hard. The few months that followed hit me like a freight train and I hadn't even seen it coming. I found myself spending a lot of time on my couch at my apartment. The Amazing TV Suit became my only source of companionship. It kept me warm when I needed it. It didn't bother me if I didn't want to talk, which was always. It was there for me no matter what. I actually started talking to it like it was not an inanimate object. I thanked it when it made me feel cozy and I apologized to it when I spilled food on it. I don't think I took it off for days at a time. All I had to do was lift it up over my waist when I needed to pee, and my arms were consistently free to move about. It was perfect. It was my friend, my shield, my comfort. I'd spent days just lying there staring at the television. I wasn't stepping foot outside. I wasn't changing out of my pajamas or even showering for that matter. I obsessed over every negative feeling I'd had. I couldn't believe how awful I felt.

I was a coward. I felt guilty. I wished that I had fought against these assholes. Better yet, I'd wished that I never let them treat me like they did in the first place. I should've been stronger. I should've stood up for myself. I couldn't believe that I settled instead of taking my case to court. On top of that, what was I going to do with my life? I had no idea where to begin with regard to a new career. I had the career counselor to look forward to, sure, but just how much help was that really going to be? What did I really want to do with my life? I suppose I was more pissed off that I had to do all of this changing in the first place. I mean, I had my life planned out for myself. I'd had it planned out for a while. I had worked so hard to get to where I was and now it was gone. How could I have dismissed my hard work so easily? I had given BSJ seven years of my life hoping to further perfect my professional self, only to get shit on by them. They turned me against them and I let them. I let them chase me out of there. I decided to leave. What was wrong with me?

I had spent months studying for all of my licenses. I had taken one exam after another and it wasn't easy for me. I'd busted my butt for nothing. It was gone. I had chosen to leave, and it was too late to turn back. Sure, I could've gone to another firm in the same industry, but at that point I knew my references wouldn't pan out, and how would I be able to explain to my future prospective employer why I left BSJ anyway? Besides, I had heard throughout this ordeal that all big financial corporations had similar cultures. I'm sure it varied from desk to desk and department to department, but what if I got somewhere else and it was the same? I actually had a hard time deciding not to go back into the financial industry, but I knew it would be a battle I wasn't prepared to fight after being worn out from fighting BSJ. At first I thought that I should take the opportunity to go a completely different route with my career. You know, doing something more rewarding where the motivation wasn't money, it was knowing you're doing something good. I thought about non-profit work or even teaching. It did seem like a good idea at first.

My thoughts quickly changed as I grew more and more disgusted with having to start all over again. I was so aggravated that wherever I went now, I'd have to start at the bottom and work my way up. That was so unfair. I was beyond the years of paying my dues and doing lower level work. Why should I have to go through all of this again? I did all of that right when I got out of college. I'd been there. What the hell was I thinking when I decided all of this? The thing was, I wasn't thinking clearly at all. I completely overlooked the fact that I'd potentially have to go back to school to get a degree in whatever it was I wanted to do. Those school days were behind me and it can be very difficult going back and I'd never thought about that. All of these thoughts were making me crazy. I couldn't focus on anything I had to do to continue my life. I was dwelling on what had been done to me, or what I had done to myself, and that was holding me back. I was swimming in my own self-pity and eventually drowned in it.

My eating was completely out of control. Living in the city had its perks. You could eat forever without ever leaving your apartment and still have every choice imaginable twenty-four hours a day seven days a week. The delivery guys from where I ordered most of my three to four meals a day were the only people I'd talk to. They knew me by my first name. It was the only human contact I'd been having. I was a good tipper and very courteous when they arrived, but I usually rushed them off because I couldn't keep the good mood charade going for more than about three minutes. Every morning I was having chocolate chip pancakes with an order of bacon well done and a large diet coke. I know, I know, what's the sense in having a diet coke, right? Well, I literally drank diet coke just for the taste of it. I switched from regular to diet back in high school and I couldn't stand the taste of regular anymore. Anyway, after devouring that down, I'd be hungry again in about two hours. That was when Chinese food was called upon to help me through my misery. I switched it up from time to time between the beef chow fun and sweet and sour chicken. Of course, no lunch was complete without the pork fried rice and two egg rolls. I would eat every last bit of it too. Each time I sat down at the living room coffee table, it was like I hadn't eaten in days.

Nighttime was different as far as what I ordered. Sometimes I'd do Thai food, other times I'd crave Italian. Whichever it was, though, sometimes it wasn't enough. There was the more than I'd care to admit frequent late-night diner order. This was the place that I usually got my pancakes from, so that meant they came to my place twice in one day. How pathetic was that? I felt so miserable most of the time except when I was eating. I told myself that it was okay to binge since it made me happy, and I deserved to feel happy since I was otherwise so depressed. But then, what I recognize now as internalized fat phobia emerged. You can imagine how awful I felt every time I was finished. I felt sick. I was disgusted with myself. But that didn't matter for the next time. I kept on doing it despite the fact that I was gaining a lot of weight so quickly. One morning I recall looking in the mirror and noticing it in my face and on my body. I must have put on about 25 lbs. I never stepped on the scale for fear of actual proof making it more real, so I wasn't certain exactly how much weight I did put on. I was literally carrying around the weight of my stress.

I hadn't realized this at first, but the medication I was on contributed to my increased appetite. I was first referred to a psychiatrist by Dr. Alice in order to get medicine to help me sleep. When I met Dr. Bennett, I was at the top of a downward spiral just ready to take the plunge. Of course, I hadn't realized it at the time, nor did he. He was a dope anyway. I hated going to see him; he didn't really seem to help me except for the fact that he wrote my prescriptions. I didn't care so much, since I still had Dr. Alice to talk to. I was seeing each of them once a week, which ended up being the only time I left my apartment those days.

I was diagnosed with insomnia immediately, and the doctor prescribed me sleeping pills. I began to abuse those pretty quickly. Once I started taking two at a time, things snowballed out of control. My body was getting used to the dosage of two, so then I had to take three and four and so on. Dr. Alice was trying to stay on top of my medications as much as possible, or so she thought. I totally lied to her about them. I told her that I was only taking one every few days. Meanwhile, Dr. Bennett prescribed me with three other medications to help me with my anxiety and depression. Dr. Alice found out soon enough and when she asked me how I felt about it all, I told her that I didn't care.

"I don't think medication is a long-term solution Elizabeth, but I do think it could be of some service in the meantime." Dr. Alice was trying to get me to talk about how I felt about being on so many different drugs.

"Yeah, it's totally fine for now. Dr. Bennett came recommended by you, so it can't be that bad, right?" She could tell I was getting irritated with her probing, yet she was extraordinarily patient with me.

"Yes, that is true, but I just don't want the medication to cover up what is really going on inside you." What did she really think could possibly happen under both her and Dr. Bennett's care?

Turns out, bad shit could happen. I had gone completely out of control and I was lying to her and everyone else about it. I hadn't told anyone else that I was seeing a psychiatrist, so when I called my mother to tell her that I wanted to go see my general practitioner, she didn't see the harm in it. I told her that I might need something to help me sleep and possibly some anti-anxiety medication. She encouraged me to talk it fully through with him. Dr. Reed was our family doctor, so she trusted him. I did too; he was a nice guy and a great physician, and so I felt kind of guilty duping him into giving me drugs. I was curious to see if I could pull it off and as soon as I did, I was on cloud nine.

I planned everything out ever so carefully. I had three of the same prescriptions from two different doctors. It was great. For a while it was like an endless supply of pills right at my fingertips. I had been going to two different drugstores to get these pills, which was ridiculously simple since there is a drugstore on every corner in the city. Actually, the medicine cabinet above my bathroom vanity eventually started resembling a drugstore. For a while there, I don't think I went a twenty-four-hour period without something in my system. I was popping Xanax, Ativan, Remeron, and Ambien like they were candy. I completely lost control and knew it but didn't care.

I was lying to my family and friends. Every word out of my mouth was deceitful. My mother was calling me regularly and I was telling her that I found a church to volunteer at in the city. I hadn't. I told her that I spent a lot of time at the career center where my counselor was, when in fact I had only been there and met the woman once. The biggest lie of all that I told was that I was doing fine. Kris and Marissa had called on several occasions to see if I'd join them for nights out on the town and I told them that I was too tired from getting up so early to get over to the church to serve the homeless people breakfast. I told them I got involved in some other projects there that were keeping me busy, and I also told them that once I figured out what I was going to do with my job situation, the volunteer stuff would subside, and I'd definitely be up for more time with them.

Apparently, I lied really well; a true sign of an addict, I suppose. The girls and my parents were all so happy for me and proud of me for overcoming what I had. It was so easy to lie since I lived alone and so far away from everyone. The only ones who were suspicious were Steve and Kristin. They invited me down the shore several times that summer following the mediation and the wedding, and I rejected each invitation. I normally would never turn down a trip to the Jersey shore. Ever. It wasn't just the beach that I loved. It was the memories I had with my friends, the boardwalk, the frozen custard, the cheesesteaks, the whole vibe. It was my happy place. So they knew something was up.

Once I actually had to clean my apartment and shower and dress because I couldn't discourage my mom from paying me a visit. I was a nervous wreck. "Elizabeth, I miss you so much and I know you're busy, but can't we just get together for lunch? I'll come to you." That was a huge deal because my mom hated to drive into the city. I knew she really needed to see me, so with much coaxing, I agreed to have her come over and we'd go to lunch.

"I will make sure I mark you in my calendar, Ma. I'm so busy these days, I can't even keep up with myself." Yeah, I was so busy lying around, popping pills, drinking, and eating I could barely make time for my own mother to come see me.

"I can't wait to see you. I'm so excited for our girls' day out. Maybe we could go to one of those day spas, too."

"Don't push it, Ma, my schedule is tight as it is." I put on my best phony joke voice.

"Alright, alright, next time." She sounded a tad disappointed, but I got over it quickly. After all, she was cutting into my loafing time enough as it was.

"Hellooooo, mother!" I sang. I put on my best game face and threw my arms open to her.

"Hey, it is so good to see you!" She gave me the tightest hug. It actually almost took my breath away for a brief moment. She slid her hands down my arms and clasped on to my hands. "Are you okay?" I nodded yes. It took her a minute to notice how straggly I guess I was. "Your eyes are bloodshot, do they itch? Could it be pink eye? Actually, they seem a little sunken in." She placed her hand on my forehead to feel for a temperature, and then brought my head to her lips. "No, you don't feel warm. Are you sure you're okay?"

"Ma, seriously, I'm totally fine. I am just doing a lot right now to keep myself busy. I don't want to have too much time on my hands, you know? Maybe I'm overdoing it a little, but it's okay." I never imagined myself uttering so many lies in one breath to my own mother.

"Okay, okay, Elizabeth. I don't want to bug you about it. This is our special day together. Let's enjoy it."

"Thanks, Ma. And believe me, if I wasn't fine, you'd be the first to know about it." The lies just kept on coming.

I had done a great job of straightening up the place before she got there. There had been days of empty food containers all over the place and the dust bunnies should have been paying rent. I was careful to hide any indication of all the different bottles of medication I had. I felt so guilty being so deceptive. I managed to make it through the afternoon with my mom. It took a lot out of me. I thought it went off without a hitch. As she was leaving, she tried to plan some time for me to come home for a while just to take it easy. "What about a few days next week? You could use the rest." She was practically begging.

"I can't, Ma. If I really want to get into non-profit work, I have to put a lot of volunteer hours in. I want to rack up enough points and make enough connections so that my transition from the business world is a smooth one." Where the hell did I come up with this crap? I was so good, I almost started believing my own lies. I guess I was delusional. I knew that all of those things I was saying were what I wanted to do, but just didn't have it together enough to do.

Immediately after she left, I ripped my clothes off, jumped

into my pajamas that could have probably put themselves on me, and curled up under my blanket on the couch. I cried and cried and cried for about five hours. Seeing my mother triggered this sadness so intense that I couldn't even control myself. After being so sick of crying, I opened a bottle of wine to help the medication take effect more quickly. I knew it was even riskier than just taking the pills, but I didn't care. I was lower than I'd ever felt, and I needed something to help me.

With each new day after that, I had less and less hope that I'd get out of this slump. I was so overwhelmed by my negative thoughts and feelings that I wanted to crawl out of my own skin. I disgusted myself more than I ever had before. Who the hell was I to feel this bad? Big deal, I had a bad work situation. It was over, why was I dwelling on anything? I felt tremendous guilt for feeling so awful about my life. I couldn't control it either. I was physically healthy, I had my family and friends who were there for me and loved me, and I had a good foundation to get my life going again. What was wrong with me? So many other people out there have had to deal with things much worse than I had. Why couldn't I just snap out of it, count my blessings and move on? I didn't get it and that made me feel worse.

I contemplated killing myself a few times. I was, however, afraid to use up too many of my precious pills in doing so. I was worried that if I didn't take enough to kill me, I would have to have enough left over for the next day if I was still alive. How warped is that? Just in case, I should've taken them all to ensure that I wouldn't wake up. I guess that was part of me not really wanting to die. Once in the middle of the night, I woke up from a brief sleep to find my face pressed against a picture of Thomas and Eddie. I didn't remember what I was doing with a photo of my nephews, but I knew I had been crying with it. It was blotched and smudged with my tears. I couldn't remember. That actually happened a lot, not remembering. Since my sleeping was scarce and scattered throughout a twenty-four-hour period, sometimes even nights and days blended together. I couldn't remember segments of time. I wouldn't remember meals I had eaten, pills I had taken, bottles of wine I had drunk or even sometimes, I couldn't remember what day it was. Oftentimes, I'd blow it off. What the hell was the sense in remembering anyway? I knew the only two places I had to be were on Monday nights to see Dr. Bennett and Wednesday nights to see Dr. Alice and that was it. I usually set my alarm clock for those appointments. I was in a daze most of the time, but I managed to pull myself together enough for my visits to them.

I would also set my alarm for ten o'clock every weekday morning. It was the only time of my day, any day, that I could feel somewhat happy. It was when I was watching the *Ellen DeGeneres Show*. It was new at the time. Sounds silly, right? It was silly and light and easy and fun, and I loved every minute of it. I swear it was the only thing I looked forward to during my really low time. I didn't quite have the energy to participate in the dance segments, of course, but I was dancing a little bit on the inside. I couldn't really explain it or understand it, but I loved feeling so good if only for a measly little hour. If it were up to me, I'd have an Ellen network where I, or anyone else who needed a pick-me-up, could watch her whenever we wanted. Sometimes I would imagine myself there at the show joining in on the fun. It was awesome. After a while, I never even had to set my alarm to make sure I as awake for it. My internal alarm clock would go off at about nine thirty no matter how little sleep I had just gotten. I'd have just enough time to order my pancakes and bacon and nestle in front of the TV. It was like I was in another world for that time. It was nice.

Chapter 16

Unfortunately, Ellen wasn't on all the time and my bad feelings overcame me so intensely, I couldn't really hide it anymore. Dr. Alice was the first to notice how severe my depression was. She expressed her concern to me and began seeing through my lies. She dealt with me so delicately. I think I might've even appreciated the fact that she knew I wasn't well. I wanted someone to rescue me. My behavior had been a cry for help. I didn't realize it at the time, but I did want someone to find out what I was doing. I was on the verge of a breakdown, a big one, and I didn't want to go through it alone. I didn't trust myself. I didn't know what extreme measures I would take. I didn't want to die more than I did want to die. I suppose that was why I started to unload on her everything I was doing. It was over the course of three sessions that I explained all of my thoughts and feelings and was truthful about what I was doing. She admitted to thinking something wasn't quite right.

"You talk about going into a zone. What kind of zone? Describe it. What is it like?" She needed to hear all of this to fully assess my situation.

"It is so hard to put into words. I mean, I sometimes can't tell the difference between what is real and what is a dream. My thoughts are all over the place." I knew that had a lot to do with all of the drugs I was taking. (I fessed up to that, by the way, and she was very good in dealing with that.) "I get scared when I realize there are bits of time I can't remember. At first, I didn't care. Now I am really getting scared and that just adds to my anxiety."

"You need some serious, intensive, structured therapy that I can't provide for you. I am extremely worried about you right now."

"What are you saying? What do you mean?" I didn't quite understand.

"I'm saying I'm checking you into a hospital. I know a great place you could go." She almost said it with a sigh of relief like she had been afraid to mention it the past three weeks. She didn't want her suggestion to push me over the edge. She didn't know whether I was going to be accepting of the treatment or blow up. She took a chance and I was glad she did.

"You have got to be fucking kidding me." Okay, okay, so I wasn't glad right away that she did it. "I am in no way comparable to people in psych wards of hospitals."

"Elizabeth," she tried to assure me that this was the right thing to do. "What you are dealing with is beyond your control. You could never get out from under this severe depression on your own. You need help."

"I am getting help, you!" I was starting to shout at her.

"I am trying to help you but cannot help you to the full extent that you need. I don't have the time or resources to devote to the level of care that you need. I wish I could, trust me."

"Ah ha, you're bailing on me." I felt betrayed yet again.

"No, no, no, Elizabeth, I promise you that I am not bailing on you. I want you to be in a place where you have nothing to do but concentrate on getting well. It'll be a safe comfortable place for you. The people there are qualified to give you round-the-clock care. I am not. It could actually be kind of nice not to worry about anything else for a while. I will help you get things started and promise to call you every single day. You even have my number if you need to call me. I will be there for you via telephone whenever you need me. We can talk whenever you want. I've worked with this hospital before, we all work well together. They know me and how I am with my patients. Please understand that I am doing this because I truly care about your wellbeing." I knew that about her. She did care about me. I just couldn't understand how she could ship me off to some mental ward filled with complete strangers.

"And where is this place?" I was still sounding skeptical intentionally. I didn't want to let on that I was minutely interested.

"It's not far away at all. It's maybe twenty minutes outside of the city," she assured me.

"Okay, this is all so crazy, can I think about it? I mean, this is a lot for me to handle right now." I was being honest, but still doubted that I'd ever agree to it. I was appeasing her.

"Alright. I will have my cell phone with me at all times for the next forty-eight hours, even at my bedside. I want to see you Friday as well this week."

"Okay." I had her explain a little more about this place. I would be checking into the crisis center at this hospital. It was not for long-term psychiatric patients. The maximum inpatient stay is two weeks and then you can stay as an outpatient as long as you feel comfortable. I was a little relieved to hear that, but it still didn't sound all that appealing. She did explain that it was a voluntary program and that nobody could come and take me away to it. None of this explanation was convincing enough for me. I wanted help, but not this kind of help.

As soon as I got home after seeing Dr. Alice that night, I truly lost it. How had my life turned into such a disaster? I knew it was my entire fault despite what Julie and Dr. Alice had been telling me. I believed they were telling me that there was nothing else I could've done just to make me feel better. Yes, I had been taken advantage of and humiliated, but I could've stopped it. I should have stopped it. I allowed these horrible things to happen to me. It was my fault, and it was still my fault that I was wallowing in sorrow. I couldn't find my inner strength to pull myself out of this. I was a weak person. None of this would have happened to a strong person.

I didn't want to deal with anything anymore. I couldn't handle what Dr. Alice was telling me about going to that "place." In the past, I had wanted to be dead. I didn't fully want to kill myself; otherwise, I would've accomplished that already. I think

I almost wanted it. I know that sounds weird, but it was difficult to explain. I wanted to be gone temporarily. I didn't want to talk to or see anyone for a while. I wanted to escape and come back when I was ready to come back. I wanted my family and friends to know why I was gone so they knew the severity of my misery. I think that night, I saw that I was going to check into the hospital, but I wasn't about to go without one last breakdown. I guess I felt I needed it.

All I can recall is standing in front of my bathroom vanity, fiercely staring at my reflection, trying to reach the depths of my soul.

There were more than a few things missing in between that point and waking up in the hospital.

"Oh my God," I looked up groggily in sheer horror. "Where are we?"

We were in the emergency room at one of the hospitals in the city and my parents, Heather, and Dr. Alice were there. I was lying in a hospital bed with a gown on and an IV in my right arm. The four of them surrounded me at the foot of my bed. Dr. Alice had their home number since my mother was my emergency contact. It turns out that she had called them to express her concerns about my condition. She delicately told them to maybe check up on me over the next few days. When they tried my apartment phone and my cell phone about eight hundred times in a matter of one hour that night, they immediately headed into the city and called Dr. Alice on the way. She met my parents at my apartment and when I hadn't answered the door, they busted it down. Thinking about it is kind of funny. My mom and Dr. Alice each stand barely five feet tall and my dad is about five six, five seven tops. They're all so little, how the hell did they get that door down? Apparently, it was my mom. My dad later told me that it only took her two full body pounds to knock the door in. Cheap old building. Good thing I was safe from burglars or other lunatics that ran around Manhattan.

"Was I bad?" I knew right away that they must have found me somewhere in my apartment completely out of it.

"You were responsive but incoherent." Dr. Alice was the only one who could actually speak about what had happened. My folks were still quite shaken up about the whole thing. My mother was quiet when she came over to hug me. She squeezed me around my head so tightly I thought it was going to burst.

"Ma, I'm fine, I'm fine! Let go." I could barely breathe. "Geez, what are you trying to kill me?" I kind of smirked and let out a teeny giggle.

"That's not funny." My mother was pissed at that comment. My father did not say one word; he just sat at the side of my bed and held my hand. He was good at it too.

"So what's the deal?" I knew what was coming.

"They'll arrange to have a bed ready for you at the wellness center if you are willing to go." Dr. Alice cut to the chase.

"Yes, yes, yes, I so want to go. I do. I just need you to tell me what to expect while I'm there." I did want to go. I wanted to go so badly. This was my escape. This was my chance to disappear for a while and come back when I was ready. Dr. Alice said that it would be good for me to just relax there and not worry about anything going on in my life. All I had to do was follow their schedule and focus on getting better.

"How long will it take for a transport?" I heard Dr. Alice speaking with one of the hospital physicians. "Okay, let's go over the details outside and give Elizabeth time alone with her family here."

"Do not even think of lecturing me right now. That's the last thing I need." I was directing that towards my parents, but Heather came over to give me a hug. I think she felt a little uncomfortable. I don't think she knew really how to act towards me. Who could blame her? It was all a bunch of uncomfortable small talk for a while until Dr. Alice came in and gave us the game plan. The ambulance was taking me, and Heather and my parents were to follow us in their car.

Dr. Alice had already spoken to the doctor at the center, so every-thing was taken care of. She thanked my parents for their help and before she left, she leaned down and gave my hand a tight squeeze.

"I'll call you first thing in the morning. You're going to do really well there. I know it." She gave me a little wink and walked out the door. I looked over at my family and they all looked relieved. I gathered that they were happy I had Dr. Alice in my life. She saved me. She really had.

Part Four

That Which Does Not Kill Me, Makes Me Stronger

Chapter 17

I was in and out of sleep the remainder of the time at the hospital and before the transport. I vaguely remember getting into the ambulance and then waking up sporadically during the twenty-minute ride over to the wellness center. At some point during the transport, and I had no idea about the specifics, my Aunt Donna ended up with my mom, and my dad and sister got my sister back home to her boys. So there I was, being wheeled in to this place on a stretcher and my mother and aunt were right next to me. It was dark out already. Where had the day gone? They switched me to a wheelchair when I got inside. I probably could have walked by that time but figured it might be protocol, so I didn't say anything and just stayed in it the wheelchair.

There was a kind looking woman in scrubs there. She was a nurse. She greeted me pleasantly at the reception desk. "Welcome, Elizabeth. We are happy to have you here and hope we can do everything to help you. Now, can I get you anything before we begin the check-in process? Would you like some water?"

"Umm," I mumbled. I was parched. "I'd actually like a coffee please?"

"Oh no, I'm sorry. We don't have that here." Oh, this poor unsuspecting woman. I mean, she might have had to deal with worse in her line of work, but telling me that I can't have a coffee is like telling a fish it can't have water. I un-leashed pure hell on her.

"WHAT DO YOU MEAN YOU DON'T HAVE ANY coffee? You can't get me any coffee? There isn't any coffee anywhere? How can you not have any coffee? I don't get it! I am literally freaking out right now." I jumped out of the wheelchair. "Okay,

okay, I'm sorry, Diet Coke will do," I said a tad bit calmer. "I'll take a Diet Coke." I was desperate. I didn't really want Diet Coke at that time, I wanted coffee. But I would've taken a Diet Coke at that point.

"No, we don't have any coffee or any Diet Coke for that matter," the woman replied.

"We will go get you some and bring it back for you," my Aunt Donna interrupted. "I'm sure we could find somewhere that is open and be back in no time, Elizabeth."

The nurse was shaking her head. "Oh no, you can't do that. No patients are allowed any caffeine during their stays. We have ginger ale."

"ALL YOU HAVE IS FUCKING GINGER ALE? ARE YOU KIDDING ME?" I'm surprised they didn't pull out the straight jacket and sedatives. "What am I going to do for two weeks without coffee or Diet Coke?" I slumped my upper body and began sobbing heavily as if I'd just lost a loved one. I knew it wasn't all because of the beverage situation and so did everyone else there. Of course my aunt still tried to talk this woman into allowing her to smuggle me in one drink.

With her Bronx accent still prevalent after all these years, she pleaded, "Come awn, it'll just be one small cawfee or can a soder. Look attuh, she's a mess, she needs this." My aunt's eyes welled up, as did my mom's, which was insane because my mother rarely cried. She always had to play the strong one.

"I'm sorry, I can't allow you to do that," the nurse replied. Good effort, Aunt Donna. I really appreciated her trying.

I wasn't exactly sure how in the world I was going to sleep in this unfamiliar place. I rarely slept okay in the comforts on my own home. It was a little eerie at night and I had this complete stranger for a roommate. She really didn't talk to me at all, which I was perfectly fine with. She seemed to have been there before. She was not a new patient. She knew the drill. She was sitting up in bed waiting for something at lights out. Within a matter of thirty seconds, a nurse walked in and handed her a pill and a small paper cup filled with water. When my roommate finished her dose, the nurse walked over to me. I placed my hand out with my palm facing up. I didn't even ask what it was. I assumed it was some sort of sleeping pill. I didn't really care at that point, I just knew I wanted to sleep. And sleep I did.

It was absolutely unbelievable. I had never had better sleep in my entire life. Plus, I woke up fully and completely refreshed. I couldn't understand it. I had sleeping pills before, why had I never slept that well? This was really potent stuff they were giving us. They didn't mess around. Not to mention, I was never, ever tired or groggy during the day. I never needed a pick me up of caffeine at 3 or 4 pm. I could sit in the quiet lounge with the warm sun beating down on me reading a book at three thirty in the afternoon and have not an inkling of drowsiness. I thought that maybe they pumped oxygen through the vents of the building during the day. I'd once heard they do that in casinos to keep you up later and gambling more money away. Is that a real thing or just a myth? Anyway, I couldn't understand it, but it felt great.

Dr. Alice called once a day like she said that she would. The first two days or so, I cried when I heard her voice. She was very calming though. My folks were allowed to visit but only for an hour in the evenings. I was also limited to two people per visit, so I could never have my folks and Heather there all at the same time, which would have been nice. I didn't cry in front of my parents like I did with Dr. Alice. I didn't want them to worry more than they already were. I knew they would.

When I first started with the art and music therapy, I thought it was a complete waste of time. Slowly but surely, I came to realize that it was absolutely delightful. A peaceful feeling came over me while I was creating or listening. I couldn't explain it, nor did I need to. I just knew it was working. It was calming.

We had group therapy once a day. The first few days of group therapy angered me. I didn't feel like I was in the right place. I didn't feel like I should be there with people who needed their blood tested regularly in order to determine amounts of medication they needed. They required the severe therapy that I didn't think, at first, I had to have. I suppose I was in denial for a while about how much help I actually required. Why did I even feel the need to compare myself to other patients? Eventually I understood that was part of the process. I had to recognize the severity of my depression and face it head on.

I basically sat silent for the first few rounds of group therapy. I observed and listened to the other patients. There was another young woman there who was rather quiet in the beginning as well. One day she slowly opened up with a pretty traumatic story slightly similar to mine. "Huh," I thought to myself. "She sounded a lot like I did." Her feelings were familiar to me. I was no stranger to what she was describing, and it felt peculiar to me. I didn't fully grasp what was happening at the time. I was beginning to understand that I was not alone in feeling what I felt. I sensed that this was one of the reasons group therapy was helpful. I began crying quietly to myself as she spoke. My overwhelming emotions flooded me. And I realized that I did need to share. I needed to talk to complete strangers about the most intimate, atrocious details and it would be okay. I felt less alone from then on. And oddly enough, a little less crazy, in a psych hospital.

All the blame that I had been putting on myself began lessening. It was not completely gone, though. I began to realize that blaming myself and dwelling on it was not helpful if I wanted to make progress. And I did want to make progress. I didn't want to alienate myself from my friends and family, eat myself out of house and home, not shower, and wallow in my misery.

Chapter 18

When my mom picked me up after my two-week stay, I was elated to step outside of that building, but I knew that I still had a long road of recovery ahead of me. It wasn't as if I felt like a prisoner there. I realized I had been imprisoning myself. I had closed myself off and shut down. I felt freer than I had in a while. My cousin Jessica, Aunt Donna's youngest, came with my mother and she brought me an extra large coffee with a big red bow on top. I hadn't even cared that my mom and aunt told her the story. In retrospect, I even was able to chuckle about it.

I was an outpatient there for two more months. At first it was every day and then it was two to three times a week. I also continued to see Dr. Alice twice a week. It was exhausting at times, since I had to drive into the city to see her. I was staying at my folks' for a while, because I didn't trust myself on my own. When my lease for my apartment in the city was up for renewal, I never renewed it and officially moved back in with my parents. It was not quite where I thought I would be at that point in my life, but I knew that I had to start over.

Throughout the healing process, I realized that it was actually good to feel the negative feelings that I had. I was usually the happy-go-lucky one who tried to be positive all the time. It wasn't real. I was burying and internalizing all that negativity and destroying myself from the inside out. Shit happens and what happened to me was really shitty. I realized that I had to sit with the shitty feelings and just feel the shit and process the shit in order to move on from the shit. Say that five times fast.

I was still anxious about what came next in my life. What

career path was I going to take? Chances are that most companies, either in finance or elsewhere, were not like BSJ, at least I'd like to think that they weren't. I'm sure most of BSJ wasn't like my group, from what I gathered. I soon came to realize that I needed an altogether different motivation. I didn't want it to be about the money anymore. I mean, let's face it, when I was paid properly, the money was awesome. But I longed for something more fulfilling and meaningful. I wanted a clean slate.

Roberta had mentioned to me once when we had an intern on our desk that I was a great teacher. She said that she'd never seen or heard anyone take the time to explain things the way I had and done it so well. I told her that I learned from the best! But she insisted that even she couldn't help but admire me for it. That stuck with me and helped me with the next phase of my life. While I still thought about doing not-for-profit work as a career, I decided against it because there were always opportunities to volunteer.

I decided to become a teacher. I always loved children and enjoyed being around them. I loved watching my nephews explore and develop. It was so amazing to me. Before my two months as an outpatient ended, I enrolled in a school close to home and commuted. Since I already had a four-year degree, albeit in business, I wasn't required to go back to school for another four years. I was able to attend a teaching certification and masters' program all in one. It would take two years to complete. I gathered that there were a lot of people out there who changed their careers like this, thus the existence of this program.

While I was going to school, I took a job as a teacher's assistant at the preschool my nephews had attended. I had been to the school several times in the past to pick them up when I was helping my sister. It was such an amazing place. It was a converted gigantic old house and it felt very warm and welcoming. The Director, Ms. Louise, was an amazingly kind and generous woman, as were most of the teachers there. A lot of the senior staff had been working there for over a decade, which proved to me that it'd be a great place to work.

Once my schooling was completed, I had to figure out where I'd find a job. It was in December, so midway through the school year. I figured that I could take on more hours at the preschool where I was assisting and look for something where I could start the following September. I specialized in early childhood education, preschool through third grade. I was willing to travel to any nearby town and was open to starting as an assistant elsewhere if I needed to. Coincidentally, one of the women who taught the four- and five-year-olds at the school where I already was had put in her notice to leave. Ms. Louise didn't hesitate to ask me if I'd replace her. It was a perfect fit and less of an adjustment for the children since most of them all knew me already. I accepted!

It was then that I decided the fun thing I wanted to do that I had been toying with since the mediation. I bought myself a gift for completing school and getting a new job. I bought my own shore house! I had always dreamed that my high paying financial career would eventually afford me the opportunity to own a shore house. And even though I was robbed of that career, I wasn't going to let that dream die. I had my very own happy place. All I wanted to do was fill it with my friends and family and create new, wonderful memories. I was elated! And even though it was the dead of winter, Steve, Kristin, and I were down at that house every weekend the first few months I had it.

Chapter 19

Like any job, of course, there were some challenges. But any bad day at the school was a million times better than the best days at my previous job. It's funny, the maturity level of the four- and five-year-olds I was working with was on par with the maturity level of the men I used to work with. But seriously, the children would sneeze on me or wipe their grimy hands on me. They were loud and they whined and cried a lot. But they needed me, they appreciated me, and they loved me. My heart was full. And even though my paycheck wasn't quite as full as it used to be, that didn't matter anymore. Money could never buy the profoundly beautiful feelings I felt while teaching and influencing these children's lives, maybe giving them something they'd hold onto forever.

I hadn't dated anyone seriously during any of this. When I first started at BSJ & Co., I was so focused on the work that I might have only gone out on a couple of dates with one or two guys. I barely got to know them and was over it. Dating still proved to be troublesome but for different reasons. It was quite nerve-wracking when I thought about being able to trust men again. I know, I know, not all men were like the men that I used to work with, but I was petrified. At that point, after all was said and done and I was settled in my new life, I knew I'd be ready to share it with someone sooner rather than later. I was happy. I was renewed. I was more true to myself than I had ever been in my life. That was worth sharing.

I was still living at home and was absolutely okay with that. I knew with this new job, I'd be out searching for a place to live closer to the school in no time. I had been getting back to normal

169

and going out with my friends again on a regular basis. I was able to crash at friends' places when we all went out. Jill and Charlie came out with my high school friends and me a few times. I even stayed at their apartment on several occasions. She and I spent a few of those nights in their apartment talking for hours after Charlie had fallen asleep. Jill and I mended our friendship, but it did take a hard hit. I don't think it was ever really the same again, but it was good nonetheless. The relationships with all of my high school friends, my group, went right back to the way it was. It was amazing and beautiful. I apologized to all of them and they wanted nothing more than for me to forget about it. They kept telling me that I didn't need to apologize and that I was traumatized and that putting up with that is what friends are for. I was so lucky to have them.

I said those exact apologies to my family, too, and they all basically responded the same way that my friends did. Everyone understood and once again I couldn't help but count my blessings. I was so lucky to have them, too. I couldn't even imagine going through what I had without all of them; even when I pushed them away.

Part of my long-term therapy and recovery was writing. Dr. Alice had suggested that it might be good for me to write about everything that happened to me. It would serve as a cathartic release of sorts. With my tendency to internalize things, getting it out and on paper could only help. It made perfect sense. I never imagined, though, that the words would come flying onto my computer so effortlessly. My mind was flooded, and the writing was pouring out. My fingers pounded the keyboard with conviction. I couldn't type faster than the thoughts running through my head. It was liberating, and I absolutely needed it to help me heal. It was an exceptional tactic for me to cope with all that I had been through. It was my story, and putting it all in writing made it so much more real. Hearing the words read aloud made me further realize how what I went through was immensely horrific. And as

I wrote, every single one of those clichés that my friends and family would sometimes reiterate started making more and more sense to me. I was, in fact, stronger. Although I didn't see it about myself at the time, I had already been strong despite this situation. The worst actually did pass, and there was a silver lining around my once very dark cloud. Things might not always turn out that way and that's alright, too. But I was determined to believe I'd be okay. I chose to believe those obnoxious clichés because that's what worked for me.

I had never really thought about what would become of my writing. At first, it started out as a journal with dates and events listed in chronological order. Then it became this book. This book, my story, sat hidden in a desk drawer for about fifteen years. And then it occurred to me that I am surely not the only woman who had gone through something like this. This is my story. Take it for what it is and if some of it is familiar in any way, maybe, at the very least, feel a little less alone. I am sharing it for that reason. So here it is.

And here I am. Years later, long after the worst of it all, I am healed and have moved on. But I also know, with certainty, that this will always be a part of me. That experience helped shape the woman I am today. I have a totally different life than I did back then and am completely fulfilled. I now have an extraordinary family of my own and I've wholeheartedly embraced my career change. I made a right turn off of Wall Street on to Sesame Street and never looked back.

Acknowledgements

To the strong and beautiful women in my life who inspire me every day, especially my mother and my sister.

Mom – For always teaching me to fight for what I believe in and leading by example. You carried me through this ordeal.

"Heather" – We speak our own language that nobody else understands. Nobody knows me better than you do. For always being my sounding board and going through everything in my life with me.

AD, C, and J – You're like having another mom and two more sisters. For helping me through this probably more than you even realize.

"Marissa," "Kristin," S, and my city girls, N and M – For being my nearest and dearest. You are my goddesses and I love you so very much. I am eternally grateful for each and every one of you.

"Dr. Alice," and "Julie" – You saved me, and you'll always hold a special place in my heart.

Sue – For helping to make all of this possible. Thank you for your support, friendship, and being my biggest cheerleader.

Stephanie – For helping to pull this all together and looking out for me.

To all of the fabulous women I didn't know at the time this was written, especially my close friends – For being awesome and loyal and dear.

To the real men in my life who inspire me every day, especially my father and my husband.

Dad – You are the most patient, selfless, and generous person I know. For your unending strength and being the person whom I aspire to be in so many ways.

D – I was lucky enough to get the family I was born into, but you are the family I chose. I chose wisely. For your endless support. I'm thankful for it and you. Everything happens for a reason. I love you. "The Big Three" always.

UE, E, and B – For being there through it all with your quiet support.

"Steve" – For being there for me, Every. Single. Day. I miss you, Every. Single. Day.

"Brian" and "Jim" – the memories we all have are priceless. For always making them funnier and better.

HJC – For your poker face.

Made in the USA
Columbia, SC
24 March 2021

34957765R00098